HE WHO HUNTED BIRDS
IN HIS FATHER'S VILLAGE

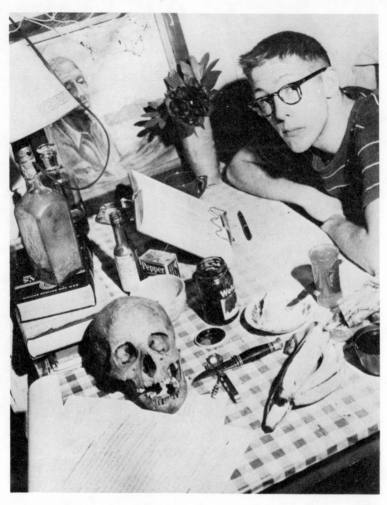

Gary Snyder at work on his thesis in 1951

GARY SNYDER

He Who Hunted Birds in His Father's Village

THE DIMENSIONS OF A HAIDA MYTH

With a Preface by Nathaniel Tarn

GREY FOX PRESS
Bolinas · California

Nathaniel Tarn's "By Way of a Preface," was first published in *Alcheringa,* No. 4, Autumn 1972.

The cover drawing is from a goose design for tatooing by Haida artist John Robson (collected by Dr. C. F. Newcombe in 1898). It is reproduced here by permission of the Ethnology Division, British Columbia Provincial Museum.

LIBRARY OF CONGRESS CATALOGING IN PUBLICATION DATA

Snyder, Gary.
        He who hunted birds in his father's village.

        Bibliography: p.152-156.
        1. Haida Indians—Legends. 2. Haida Indians—Religion and mythology. 3. Indians of North America—British Columbia—Legends. 4. Indians of North America—British Columbia—Religion and mythology. I. Title

E99.H2S6   299'.7   78-16935
ISBN 0-912516-37-2
ISBN 0-912516-38-0 pbk.

CONTENTS

FOREWORD

I

By mouth, by belly.

We know an oral literature helps shape a culture; is, thus, "conditioning"—it closes around a child, makes her a "Haida"—it narrows her theoretically infinite choices of what to be. And we know this to be inevitable. But already something else is at work. The oral traditions of the world (and our civilized literatures in their debt) carry within them the seeds of the self o'er-leaping. The stories we hear as children do put us in place and give us models and possibilities to dream after; before long we *are* Amish or Hopi or Jew or Atheist Radical White Kid. But the stories keep on going: they carry themes from the whole world and all human time in them, and though the child be Haida, she could travel the planet about and recognize parts of tales she'd heard everywhere.

And the stories still keep going. We do have one mind and that mind has its own ways of opening. The more familiar modern way is, great philosopher / saviour / sage / guru / Buddha / prophet individuals appear to amaze and impress and instruct us. They do this by being elevated—but not too much—and looking back this way to tell us their stories and instructions. The older way, and maybe the best, is one that isn't even noticed. Original Mind speaks through little myths and tales that tell us how to *be* in some specific ecosystem of the far-flung world—a foggy island, a chilly *altiplano*—as we sit us down around the fire. We hear of a world above and a slippery tree or pole you can climb to get there; of worlds below and mud-people dancing in the dark, of people and animals shifting shapes about, and of the need for compassion and patience and forbearance in winning aid from an ally like Mouse Woman.

To go beyond and become what—a seagull on a reef? Why not. Our nature is no particular nature; look out across the beach at the gulls. For an empty moment while their soar and cry enters your heart like sunshaft through water, you are that, totally. We do this every day. So this is the aspect of mind that gives art, style, and self-transcendence to the inescapable human plantedness in a social and eco-logical nexus. The challenge is to do it well, by your neigh-bors and by the trees, and maybe once in a great while we can get where we see through the same eye at the same time, for a moment. That would be doing it well. Old tales and myths and stories are the kōans of the human race.

II

This essay was written some years ago when I was a green would-be scholar in Oregon. I set myself to the task of laying out the many levels of meaning a single myth could hold according to the more influential contemporary modes of studying folklore. Since the several fields of study invoked here were and are often out of touch with each other, the "dimensions" discovered can easily be mutually contradictory, as well as possibly downright wrong. So, this essay is about twentieth century occidental thinking as much as Dream Time, the Old Ways, or the Haida.

What I'd emphasize now, even more than I did when I wrote it, is the primacy of performance: in the dark room, around the fire, children and old people, hearing and joying together in the words, the acting and the images. It's there that the shiver of awe and delight occurs, not in any dry analysis of archetypes or motifs—or the abstractions of the structuralist.

I went on to other modes of study and writing, but never forgot what I learned from this work. Folklorists and anthropologists have done bins of research and writing since then, but somehow nobody has yet followed through with a multidimensional approach. So I publish it finally, with its many flaws, and the encouragement of Donald Allen, hoping it will push others more trained than I, to do the work that will show how deeply important the world heritage of story is to all of us, now and always. And, to again point out that all peoples in all places share in a rich prehistoric international lore—no group is "culturally deprived" until oppressed by an invader or exploiter. The *indigenas* are bearers of the deepest insights into human nature, and have the best actual way to live, as well, May this be realized before they are destroyed.

A curse on monocultural industrial civilization and its almost deified economic and political systems that compete, exploit, and then give vast wealth and power to a tiny few while draining and scattering the cultural and natural wealth of our planet, I say.

My thanks again to Lloyd Reynolds and David French, teachers and advisors when I did this work as part of graduating from Reed College in 1951.

And one more point. In scholarship we often don't understand ourselves well enough to know why we *really* do something. The one dimension of the myth "He Who Hunted Birds in His Father's Village" that I somehow didn't clearly state, was that it's a story of lost love.

GARY SNYDER
25:IV:40078

BY WAY OF A PREFACE

It was Pound, I believe, who suggested that the diminutive number of worthwhile theses be boiled down into paragraphs and microfilmed, the rest consigned to the trash can. Or something to that effect. In an influential poet's earliest work, however, one may find the roots of later flowerings. No further reason is required for publishing *He Who Hunted Birds in His Father's Village: The Dimensions of a Haida Myth*.

Gary Snyder's thesis was presented to the Division of Literature and Language, and to the Division of History and Social Sciences, in partial fulfillment of the requirement for a degree of Bachelor of Arts, at Reed College, Oregon, in June 1951. It is a short, elegant and confident document, little afflicted by the kind of "padding and waffle" characteristic of the genre. Snyder selects a relatively simple myth from the Haida people of the Northwest Pacific Coast of British Columbia. It is about a chief's son who marries a supernatural goose-woman, loses her as the result of a social faux-pas on his people's part, looks for her with the help of a number of other supernaturals, finds her by climbing to the sky, becomes tired of that high place and is brought back to earth by Raven, becoming a seagull on some rock near to his original home. Snyder works outwards from this myth, paces us through its relation to Haida culture, and then sails out confidently into the universal dimensions of the myth—seeing it as a variant of the Swan-Maiden story so popular in various folklores—to end with what is little less than a statement of his own poetic intentions. At the time, all of us, in anthropology, were reading just about the same things: but as well as Stith Thompson or Abraham Kardiner, we meet here with Robert Graves, Freud, Jung and Joseph Campbell, not to mention T. S. Eliot, Maud Bodkin, I. A. Richards and Northrop Frye.

Had Snyder been more aware of Lévi-Strauss at the time, he might have known "The Sorcerer and His Magic" or the essay on myth in Sebeok's Indiana symposium and he might have seen that the science of myth he prefigures so well in his thesis was in fact about to break on the discipline's horizon. Had the thesis been written today, after the publication of "La Geste d'Asdiwal," the whole account would probably have been transformed. For in the Tsimshian story of the culture-hero Asdiwal, we meet again, and far more fully, with many of the themes in Snyder's Haida myth. The wife coming to the husband's father's village; the importance of starvation in setting the myth in motion; the ascent to the sky and the hero's dissatisfaction; the supernatural helpers; the tests set by the wife's father; the virtual petrification of the hero at the end—all this, even down to the role of Mouse Woman as a go-between (none of which, be it said, escapes Snyder's keen attention)—all this figures prominently in the Asdiwal saga and would have led the poet to more sophisticated comparative conclusions. The comparison of myth-item to myth-item would have given way to one of [myth-item/society] with [myth-item/society] and the search for myth's social function would have been lifted out of the naive state prevalent at that time and very probably been given a structuralist interpretation. But if structuralism's theorems were within Snyder's grasp as Moses was sighting the nearby promised land, it doesn't necessarily follow that myth research outside of them is now invalid. A major value of the thesis today could well be as a text in literature classes where myth is taken on as a study.

In this perspective, I take a few paces towards Snyder the poet in embryo within his academic work. And leap straight into *Myths and Texts*.

To begin with, as one had suspected, Indians everywhere: Ray Wells and his gelded ponies in "Logging," no. 11; Drinkswater, Crazy Horse and their apocalyptic visions (no. 12); the making of the horn spoon of the Kwakiutl ("Hunting," no. 5); Marius Barbeau's Bella Coola tribe and Irving Hallowell's Bear-cult material (no. 6); the Shuswap tribe (no. 7); dancing on the mountains (no. 8); carrying deer-fawns in the mouth (no. 10); "What will you do with human beings?" (no. 11); "that was a Kwakiutl woman" (no. 14); girls with gazelles and wolf-cubs in their arms (no. 16). In the section called "Burning," where the West shades more and more into the Asiatic East—Red Hand nevertheless in no. 6; Coyote and Earthmaker in no. 11, the Nootka in no. 13; the Mohave in 13 also and elsewhere.

Wherever he went on the West Coast, the tides came rippling into the poems, the amorous sea carried ghosts from the Northwest tribes featured in the thesis. For Snyder (so often) love is liquid, made in water. Whales blow at the sight of this Canadian Pacific; we meet them first in "Logging," no. 12:

> I ought to have eaten
> Whale tongue with them.
>   they keep saying I used to be a human being
> "He-at-whose-voice-the-Ravens-sit-on-the-sea."

But they also seem to be in the first poem of "Hunting" where the shaman kicks loose bones (climbing the pole to the sky?); in the second, with the opposition of sea-hunter to land-hunter so strong in the Asdiwal myth; in the fourth, containing perhaps the most direct allusion to Snyder's Haida myth ("the seagrass, the seagrass") and in the ninth: "Marrying women to whales." We shall have to wait for *The Back Country*, though, for a full reference to the thesis, in the heartbreak of the poem entitled "For the Boy who was Dodger Point Lookout Fifteen Years Ago":

> The snowmelt pond, and Alison,
> half-stoopt bathing like
> Swan Maiden, lovely naked,
> ringed with Alpine fir and
> gleaming snowy peaks. We
> had come miles without trails,
> you had been long alone.

The basic themes of Snyder's work, many of which appear in filigree in the thesis, are all set out in *Myths & Texts*, he grows concentrically like the great pines of the Pacific Nation which pierce his poems and give them armatures. Writing of Matriarchy and the Mother-goddess, in the thesis, Snyder moves towards her, classically, in *Myths & Texts* before she transmutes into the beautiful and terrible Kali of the Eastern Way. In the epigraph, she is "the great / Goddess Diana"; in "Logging," no. 1: she is Io, the moon-heifer; she rises, in no. 10, at her temple on Nemi, and, in no. 14, all the sacred groves are brought together from all the significant geographies: Greece, Japan, the Northwest Coast. Then, we move, under the Hindu-Buddhist aegis, to "Burning," no. 7, in which the isolation of personal love is comforted by the togetherness of love for the Earth:

> "Earthly Mothers and those who suck
> the breasts of earthly mothers are mortal—
> but deathless are those who have fed
> at the breast of the Mother of the Universe."

Leaving Actaeon to see "Dhyana in the Spring"

("Burning," no. 13) and the dark omens of ambivalent love, let's lead back to the fourteenth poem in "Logging." The "Trees down / Creeks choked, trout killed, roads" are "Bulldozed by Luther & Weyerhaeuser": the Christian menace, to be skirted by and by, to be refused by the simple act of turning one's back and moving onto more fertile philosophies, the Christian menace is here, the same old "rip-off," killing both land and people, destroying produce:

> What bothers me is all these stumps:
> What did they do with the wood?
> Then Xtians out to save souls and grab land
> "They'd steal Christ off the cross
>   if he wasn't nailed on"
> The last decent carpentry
> Ever done by Jews.
> ("Logging," no. 10)

Is it too much to see this destructive impetus at work also in the factories of Acanemia, the Ph.D. sausage machines, which Snyder was already turning away from? They are visible all through here, "the ancient, meaningless / Abstractions of the educated mind" and the "Summer professors" ("Logging," no. 5); "All these books" ("Burning," no. 2); "a city crowded with books . . . reading all morning in alleys" (no. 12) and "Steep towns, flat towns, even New York, / And oceans and Europe & libraries & galleries" (no. 15), while the truth of the object is not in books at all:

> Raven
>   on a roost of furs
> No bird in a bird-book,
>   black as the sun.
> ("Hunting," no. 4)

But the ensuing sterility—"a seed pod void of seed"—moves toward the resolution which will be developed in all the subsequent workings. The poet will wait until the next blaze and, in the meantime,

> "The brush
> May paint the mountains and streams
> Though the territory is lost."
>
> ("Logging," no. 15)

The turning of one's back, the reversal of the waters, is suggested here also: against the destruction and killing are set the pity and compassion:

> Buddha fed himself to tigers
> & donated mountains of eyes
>   (through the years)
> To the blind,
>   a mountain-lion
> Once trailed me four miles
> At night and no gun
> It was awful, I didn't want to be ate
>   maybe we'll change.
>
> ("Hunting," no. 14)

—a poem I heard him resolve at Notre Dame, only last year, saying it would be marvelous to die being eaten by a great predator. . . .

Modulated into Politics, this switchback theme prefigures the revolutions within revolutions which the poet of the sixties was to formulate in *Regarding Wave*: conservation in Nature, radicalism in Society, a program for Young America. In "Burning," no. 9, Bodhidharma, Lenin, Hsüan Tsang, Chief Joseph, Crazy Horse, Confucius and Lao-Tzu are "Forming the New Society / Within the shell of the old."

Meantime Snyder sits

> . . . without thoughts by the log-road
> Hatching a new myth
> Watching the waterdogs
>   the last truck gone."
>
> ("Hunting," no. 1)

The mythology he has announced in the closing pages of his thesis is burning. Switching "Myth is a reality lived" to "Reality is a Myth lived," Snyder closes the thesis with an apologia for the concrete unit, examined at every facet, like a diamond. "There digge!" is his final injunction.

A last word, perhaps, on language. Snyder's success: an astonishing blend of the via negativa and the via positiva, but mainly, shall we say, the former as a starting point?

> form—leaving things out at the right spot
> ellipse, is emptiness
>> these ice-scoured valleys
>> swarming with plants
>>>> (*Earth House Hold*, p. 5)

Although hatching the new myth, for a poet, is words and the relations between words. In the thesis, Snyder comments on the sudden, apparently illogical jumps that the Haida myth takes along its way and states that such leaps from topic to topic are more acceptable to readers who have known Joyce, Eliot, Mann and Kafka. In language, Snyder has learned from contemporary poetics as well as the Chinese and Japanese poets, but also perhaps from the imagination in movement of the myths he worked on as a student.

From Anthropologist to Informant: A Field Record of Gary Snyder, Form Two: Santa Fe, N.M., to Nederland, Colorado, 7.20-22,1971

NATHANIEL TARN

CHAPTER I

THE MYTH

HE WHO HUNTED BIRDS IN HIS FATHER'S VILLAGE[1]
(Told by Walter McGregor of the Sealion-town people)

He was a chief's son. He wore two marten-skin blankets,
one over the other.[2] After he had shot birds for some time
he went along among some bull pines, which stood in an
open space behind the town and presently heard geese[3] calling. Then he went thither. Two women were bathing in a
lake. On the shore opposite two goose skins hung over a
stick. The roots of their tails were spotted with white.

After he had looked a while he ran quickly (to them).
He sat down on the two skins. Then they asked him for
their (skins). He asked the best looking to marry him. The
other said to him: "Do not marry my younger sister. I am
smarter. Marry me." "No; I am going to marry your younger sister." Now she agreed. "Even so, marry my younger
sister. You caught us swimming in the lake our father owns.
Come, give me my skin." Then he gave it to her. She put

her head into it as she swam in the lake. Lo, a goose swam about in the lake. It swam about in it making a noise.

Then she flew. She was unwilling to fly away from her younger sister. After she had flown about above her for a while, she flew up. She vanished through the sky. Then he gave her (the other) one marten-skin blanket and went home with her. He put his wife's skin between two heads of a cedar standing at one end of the town. He entered his father's house with her.

The chief's son had a wife. So his father called the people together for the marriage feast. They gave her food. Instead (of eating it) she merely smelled it. She ate no kind of human food.

By and by her mother-in-law steamed some *tcal*.[4] But she liked that. While her mother-in-law was yet cooking them she told her husband to tell her to hurry. They put some before her. She ate it all. Then they began giving her that only to eat.

One day, when he was asleep, he was surprised to find that his wife's skin, after she came in and lay down, was cold. And, when the same thing happened again, he began watching her. He lay as if asleep. He felt her get up quietly. Then she went out, and he also went out just after her. She passed in front of the town. She went to the place where her skin was kept. Thence she flew away. She alighted on the farther side of a point at one end of the town.

Then he went thither quickly. She was eating the stalks of the sea grass which grew there. As the waves broke in they moved her shoreward. He saw it. Then she flew up to the place where her (feather) skin had been kept. And he entered the house before her. Then he lay down where they had their bed, after which his wife lay down cold beside him.

They became nearly starved in the town. One day the woman said to him from the place where she was sitting: "Now my father has sent down food to me." Behind the town geese were coming down making a great noise, and she went thither. They went with her. All kinds of good food lay there such as *tcal* and wild clover roots. They brought them away. For this her father-in-law called in the people.

When this was gone she said the same thing again: "Now my father is bringing food down to me." Geese again made a great noise coming down behind the town and she went thither. Again heaps of food of all kinds lay around, and they carried that also out. For that, too, her father-in-law called together the people.

At that time someone in the town said: "They think a great deal of goose food." The woman heard it. Immediately she went off. Her husband in vain tried to stop her. She went off as one of a strange family would. In the same way he tried to stop her in front of the town. She went to the place where her skin was. She flew up. She flew around above the town for a while. Her heart was not strong to fly away from her husband. By and by she vanished through the sky.

Then her husband began to walk about the town wailing. By and by he entered the house of an old man at one end of the town and asked him: "Do you know the trail that leads to my wife?" "Why, brave man, you married the daughter of a supernatural being too great for people even to think of." At once he began bringing over all sorts of things to him. After he had given him twisted cedar limbs, a gimlet, and bones,[5] he said to him: "Now, brave man, take oil. Take two wooden wedges also. Take as well, a comb, thongs, boxes of salmon eggs, the skin of a silver salmon, the point of a salmon spear." After he had got all these he came to him. "Old man, here are all the things you told me to take." "Now, brave man, go on. The trail runs inland behind my house."

Then he started in on it. After he had gone on for a while he came to some one who was looking upon himself for lice. Every time he turned around the lice fell off from him. After he had looked at him unobserved for a while he said to him: "Now brave man, do not tickle me by looking at me.[6] It was in my mind that you were coming." Then he came out to him and combed his head. He also put oil on it. He cleared him of lice. He gave the comb and the hair oil to him. Then he said to him: "This trail leads to the place where your wife is."

He started along the trail. After he had gone on for a while (he saw) a mouse with cranberries in its mouth going along before him. She came to a fallen tree. She could not get over it. Then he took her by the back with his fingers and put her across. Her tail was bent up between her ears (for joy), and she went on before him. Presently she went among the stalks of a clump of ferns.

Now he rested himself there. Something said to him: "The chief-woman asks you to come in." Then he raised the ferns. He stood in front of a big house. He entered. The chief-woman was steaming cranberries. She talked as she did so. Her voice sounded sharp. And, after she had given him something to eat, Mouse Woman said to him: "You helped me when I went to get some poor cranberries from a patch I own. I will lend you what I wore when I went hunting when I was young."

Then she brought out a box. After she had opened a nest of five boxes, she took out of the inmost a mouse skin with small, bent claws. And she said to him: "Practice wearing this." And, although it was so small, he entered it. It went on easily. Then he climbed around upon the roof of the house inside. And Mouse Woman said to him again: "You know how to use it. Now go on."

Again he set out upon the trail. After he had gone along for a while he heard someone grunting under a heavy burden. Then he came to the place. A woman was trying to carry off a pile of large, flat stones upon her back. The twisted cedar limbs she had kept breaking. After he had looked at her for a while he went out to her. "Say, what are you doing?" Then the woman said: "They got me to carry the mountains of the Haida Island. I am doing it."

Then he took out his thongs and said to her: "Let me fix it." And he bound the thongs around it. He said to her, "Now carry it on your back," and she carried it. It did not break. Then the woman said to him, "Now brave man, thank you for helping me. The trail to your wife's place runs here."

Then he set out upon it. After he had gone on for a while he came to a hill in an open place on top of which rose something red.[7] Then he went to it. Around the bottom of this something lay human bones. There was no way in which one could go up. Then he entered the mouse skin and rubbed salmon eggs before him (on the pole). He went up after it. When he stood on top of this he clambered up on the sky.

There, too, there ran a trail, and he started off upon it. After he had gone on for a while he heard the noise of laughter and singing. After he had gone on a while longer (he came to where) a big stream flowed down. Near it sat Eagle. On the other side also sat Heron. Above sat Kingfisher. On the other side sat Black Bear. He (black bear) had no claws. He said to Eagle: "Grandfather, lend me some claws." Then he lent him some. At that time he came to have claws.

After he had sat there for a while a half-man came vaulting along.[8] He had only one leg and one arm. He had but half a head. He speared silver salmon in the river and pulled them in. Then he entered his silver salmon skin and swam up to meet him. When he speared him he could not pull him down. Then he cut his string. And the half-man said: "What did it is like a human being."

Now he came to him. "Say, did something pull off your spearpoint?" "Yes," he said to him. Then he gave him the one he had. That was Master Hopper, they say. After he had gone up (he came upon) two large old men who had come after firewood. They were cutting at the trunks of rotten trees and throwing the chips into the water, when silver salmon went down in a shoal.

He went behind and put stones in from behind, and their wedges were broken off. Then he (one) said: "Alas, they will make trouble for us." Then he went and gave them his two wedges. They were glad and said to him: "This house is your wife's."

Then he went out (to it). He went and stood in front of the house. His wife came out to him. Then he went in with her. She was glad to see her husband. And all the things they gathered he, too, gathered along with them.

After he had been there for some time he came to dislike the place. And his wife told her father. Then his father-in-law called the people. In the house he asked them: "Who will take my son-in-law down?" And Loon said: "I will put him near my tail, dive into the water right in front with him, come up at the end of his father's village, and let him off." Then they thought he was not strong enough for it.

Then he asked again. Grebe said the same thing. Him, too, they thought not strong enough to do it. Then Raven said that he would take him down. And they asked him: "How are you going to do it?" "I will put him into my armpit and fly down with him from the end of the town. When I get tired I will fall over and over with him." Then they thought he could do it.

They stood in a crowd at the end of the town looking at him. He did with him as he had said. When he became very tired and was nearly down he threw him off upon a reef which lay there. "Yuwaiya, what a heavy thing I am taking down." Shortly he (the man) was making a noise there as a seagull.[9]

2. ABSTRACT OF THE MYTH

The abstract is designed to provide an easy way to refer to sections of the myth. Wherever references are made to the abstract (by such designation as "II.5") the total content of the myth-section it summarizes is implied.

I.   THE GOOSE GIRL

1.   The Hero is a chief's son. He wears two marten-skin blankets.
2.   He hunts birds among bull pines.
3.   While hunting, he hears geese calling. He discovers two goose girls bathing in a lake, with their goose skins hung up on the bank.
4.   He asks the younger sister, who is better looking, to marry him in return for her goose skin. Although the elder sister offers herself as being smarter, he insists on the younger.
5.   He returns with his bride to his father's house. He is given a marriage feast.
6.   The goose-girl bride will eat no human food, until her mother-in-law steams *tcal* for her.
7.   She puts on her skin at night and eats stalks of the sea grass.
8.   The people in the town nearly starve. The goose wife's father sends *tcal* and wild clover roots for the people.
9.   Someone says, "They think a great deal of goose food." This makes the wife reluctantly leave.

II.   SEARCH FOR LOST WIFE

1.   The husband walks about town wailing. An old man tells him he has married a daughter of a supernatural being.
2.   He brings gifts to the old man. In return the old man tells him the trail to the land of his wife, and what useful objects to take along.
3.   He meets Lice Man on the trail. To be seen by a human being tickles Lice Man. The hero helps him rid himself of lice with comb and oil.
4.   He meets Mouse Woman carrying cranberries in her mouth, needing help. In return for help, Mouse Woman gives him a mouse skin from the inmost box of a nest of five boxes. He learns how to use the mouse skin.

5. He meets a woman carrying the stones of the mountains of Haida Island. He fixes her pack with thongs. Proceeds on trail.

6. He comes to the pole extending to the sky. Climbs it as a mouse, with the aid of salmon eggs smeared on the pole.

7. He meets Eagle, Heron, Kingfisher, and Black Bear in the sky-land. Eagle gives Black Bear claws.

8. He meets half-man, who is spearing salmon in the river. He steals half-man's spearpoint in his salmon skin. Returns to human form, keeps Master Hopper's spearpoint and gives him another.

9. The hero meets two old men chopping firewood. They throw chips from rotten trunks into a river. The chips turn into silver salmon. He breaks the old men's wedges without their knowledge, then gains their gratitude by giving them another set. They tell him the location of his wife's house.

10. He is reunited with his wife, and accepted by her people.

III. THE RETURN

1. He comes to dislike the place. Father-in-law asks who will take his son-in-law down. Loon and Grebe offer to bear him near the tail but are judged too weak. Raven offers to carry him in his armpit. They think he can do it.

2. Raven becomes very tired when almost down and throws the hero off on a reef. He becomes a seagull.

CHAPTER II

THE MYTH AND THE CULTURE

1. THE METHOD

This myth has been selected from the traditional oral literature of the Skidegate group of the Haida Indians. For these people, it was uniquely their own property. It was told in their own language, by tribal members who were acquaintances, as well as storytellers. Some individuals might have heard it many times during their lives, with minor changes and variations introduced by different storytellers, but it was to them always essentially the same—meaningful in terms of their life experience and peopled by beings familiar in literature and religion who used the tools and economic techniques of everyday living. This text represents, furthermore, the essentially correct way of telling "He Who Hunted Birds in His Father's Village." To the Haida, any version which deviated far from this would be foreign and wrong.

For the comparative anthropologist or folklorist, however, it is merely one variant of an immense body of tales similar enough to be grouped under one heading, "Swan Maidens," distributed all over the world.

> . . . the story of the Swan Maidens who put off their clothing on the shore of a lake, assume human form, and are compelled to marry the hero who takes away their clothing,—(is) common property of America, Asia, and Europe. The variations are considerable; and their complexity is not so great, nor their geographical distribution so continuous, as to claim that proof of their identity has been established.[1]

The "Swan-Maiden" story has usually been told by people who knew nothing of its worldwide distribution, and who in most instances believed it to be as permanent a feature of tribal life as the annual recurrence of springtime. Every myth and tale is merely one aspect of the total life of a culture, integrated in varying degrees with other factors, and changing as other elements change. A culture's mythology is useful in providing a description of methods of fishing, or the construction of deadfalls, as well as fundamental themes and values. The study of an oral literature can be regarded, by this approach, as simply one of a number of areas one must investigate to get an understanding of a whole culture. The knowledge gained thereby works two ways, and by such research the content of a myth—the meaning it holds for the people who tell it—can be partially discovered.

The method used here is similar to that of the "sociological" literary critics. The contention that no literature can be studied apart from its milieu is well-known, and although it has had periods of unpopularity as a critical dictum, no one would seriously deny that even within Western culture sociological criticism applied with finesse can clarify problems of content in material dealing with different social classes or periods.

In studying the oral literature of a people so alien in language and custom as the Haida, some attempt to fit it into the fabric of the culture is the beginning of understanding. The principle of Franz Boas, whose theoretical formulations concerning all aspects of northwest coast culture underly this chapter, is simple: "The expression of the cultural life of the people contained in their tales gives to them a marked individuality, no matter what the incidents constituting the tales may be."[2]

In this chapter I will present a brief outline of the culture area, outline the culture traits contained in the myth, describe the Haida culture in more detail, and then analyze the myth in these terms.

2. THE NORTHWEST COAST

The aboriginal inhabitants of the coast of the northwestern United States, British Columbia, and southeastern Alaska, developed a complex way of life unlike the rest of North American Indian culture. Only the most basic traits of material culture were shared with inland groups. It was the only culture area in the world to survive into modern times with a nonagricultural economy producing a large surplus.

Part of this unique development can be related to the northwest coast itself: from Puget Sound northward, it is a maze of islands, deeply indented fjords, natural waterways and inlets; the land rising abruptly from sea level to alpine mountain life zones.

> It will be readily seen then that on such a coast because of the large number of inlets and the innumerable islands the shore is very long. This is in very great contrast with the coast of California, where the islands are few, and the coast so abrupt that the tide flows but a short distance up the rivers. On the whole, the northwest coast of America is an exceedingly favorable region for the development of a culture almost entirely dependent upon canoes for travel and transportation and upon the sea for its food supply. The sheltered channels are so continuous that the larger dug-out canoes can be brought quite safely from Skagway, at the mouth of the Chilkat River,

to the southern end of Puget Sound, provided the weather is favorable for crossing the two or three more exposed stretches of water.[3]

The climate is rainy and temperate. The high mountain ranges precipitate most of the water-bearing clouds from the Pacific in the coastal regions, and the Japan current moderates the weather—keeping the average temperatures much higher than in corresponding inland latitudes. The heavy rains have created immense "rain forests" on the mountain slopes, with almost impenetrable undergrowth in some regions. Large stands of yellow cedar (*Chamaecyparis nootkatensis*) in the north and red cedar (*Thuja plicata*) in the south provided timber for canoes, houses, and numerous household items. Other important trees are western hemlock, Douglas fir, and Sitka spruce.

> Along rocky points where it is difficult for large trees to maintain themselves, madronas or arbutus and a few oaks are found. In the river bottoms are large areas where alder and cottonwood predominate. Everywhere in the forest there is a heavy undergrowth of blueberry and huckleberry bushes, of vine maple, thimbleberries, and salmon berries. . . .
>
> Ferns tend to take the place of grasses which are practically unknown, except in the swamps, but a heavy growth of moss forms a thick carpet underfoot and covers the branches of trees.[4]

Larger land mammals are black bear, grizzly, elk (wapiti), deer and mountain goat. "Sea mammals were of much greater importance to the economic life than land mammals; the chief of these were the whale, seal, sea lion, and porpoise."[5] The chief source of food was fish, and first among fish, salmon. During the annual spring runs, when salmon crowded the rivers, a year's supply was obtained. The combination of plentiful salmon and tall, straight-grained cedars growing at water's edge—where they could be burned out at the base and toppled into the water to be towed to towns for craftsmen to work on—provided the "foundations of northwest coast culture."[6]

The total area, from northern California to Prince William Sound, has been classified by Clark Wissler in his chapter on the "Classification of Social Groups according to their Cultures" as the "North Pacific Coast Area." His characterization of the basic cultural features is compact and fairly complete:

> This culture is rather complex and presents highly individualized tribal variations; but can be consistently treated under three subdivisions: (a) the northern group, Tlingit, Haida, and Tsimshian; (b) the central group, the Kwakiutl tribes and the Bellacoola; and (c) the southern group, the Coast Salish, the Nootka, the Chinook, Kalapooian; Waiilatpuan, Chimakuan, and some Athapascan tribes. The first of these seem to be the type and are characterized by: the great dependence upon sea food, some hunting upon the mainland, large use of berries; dried fish, clams and berries are the staple food; cooking with hot stones in boxes and baskets; large rectangular gabled houses of upright cedar planks with carved posts and totem poles; travel chiefly by water in large, sea-going dug-out canoes, some of which had sails; no pottery or stone vessels, except mortars; baskets in checker, those in twine reaching a high state of excellence among the Tlingit; coil basketry not made; mats of cedar bark and soft bags in abundance; the Chilkat, a Tlingit tribe, specialized in the weaving of a blanket of goat hair; there was no true loom, the warp hanging from a bar, and weaving with the fingers, downward, clothing rather scanty, chiefly of skin, a wide basket hat (only one of the kind on the continent and apparently for rain protection); feet usually bare but skin moccasins and leggings were occasionally made; for weapons the bow, club, and peculiar dagger, no lances; slat, rod and skin armor; wooden helmets, no shields; practically no chipped stone tools, but nephrite or green stone used; wood work highly developed, splitting and dressing of planks, peculiar bending for boxes, joining by securing with concealed stitches, high development of carving technique; work in copper may have been aboriginal, but, if so, very weakly developed; decorative art is conspicuous, tending to realism in carved totem poles, house posts, etc.; some geometric art on baskets, but woven baskets tend to be realistic; each family

expresses its mythical origin in a carved or painted crest; the tribe of two exogamic divisions with maternal descent; society organized as chiefs, nobles, common people, and slaves; a kind of barter system in which the leading units of value are blankets and certain conventional copper plates; a complex ritualistic system by which individuals are initiated into the protection of their family guardian spirits, those so associated with the same spirit forming a kind of society; mythology characterized by the Raven legends.[7]

The elements cited by Kroeber as being unique to Northwest Coast culture in North America are plank houses, ornamental twining, caste stratification, slavery, potlatch credit system, and barefootedness.[8] The dominant drive of the various tribes has been described as the desire to amass wealth in order to gain prestige. The potlatch appears to be central to the organization of economic techniques, and the preservation of values inherent in the complicated system of distributing wealth, with concomitant increase of social prestige and the expected eventual return of all goods. Ruth Benedict, who sees the Northwest Coast culture as "Dionysian" and megalomaniac-paranoid by Western standards, puts the potlatch system at the root of the cultural pattern:

> These tribes did not use wealth to get for themselves an equivalent value in economic goods, but as counters of fixed value in a game they played to win. They saw life as a ladder of which the rungs were the titular names with the owned prerogatives that were vested in them. Each new step upward on the ladder called for the distribution of great amounts of wealth, which nevertheless were returned with usury to make possible the next elevation to which the climber might aspire. . . .
>
> This primary association of wealth with the validation of nobility titles is, however, only a part of the picture. The distribution of property was rarely so simple as this. The ultimate reason why a man of the Northwest Coast cared about the nobility titles, the wealth, the crests, and the prerogatives lays bare the mainspring of their culture; they used them in a contest in which they sought to shame their rivals.[9]

In this tangle of mutually unintelligible languages, warring tribes seeking to enslave each other, living in tiny villages scattered through thousands of miles of tortuous coastlines, and sharing a universal concern with wealth and prestige, the Haida stand out as most typical. "Though geographically near the extreme northern boundaries of the area, culturally they represent the focal point of Northwest Coast culture."[10] The Haida live in the Queen Charlotte Islands, forty miles off the northwest coast of British Columbia. The total area of the islands—two large and numerous smaller ones—is nearly four thousand square miles. The land rises to an altitude of 3,500 feet in the interior. "The temperature ranges between a monthly mean of 35° in January and 57° in August."[11] Here, as on the mainland, heavy rains produce immense forests. Most of the fauna of the mainland is found excepting mountain goats and other alpine-zone life. Murdock describes the Haida:

> Powerfully built but graceful, the men average five feet seven inches in stature, the women five inches less. The Haidas have broad heads (cephalic index 81), brown eyes, broad faces with prominent cheek bones, and medium or mesorrhine noses (nasal index 74). Their black hair is thick, coarse, and straight on the head, but scanty on the face and body. Their complexions, though coppery in tone, are scarcely darker than in the average European and rosy cheeks are common.[12]

The Haida spend more time in deep-sea fishing than their mainland neighbors; the halibut rivals salmon as basic fish, and their fishing equipment and canoes are the most highly developed of the area.

Haida speech is classified by Edward Sapir in his "proposed classification"—which has yet to be improved upon, although admittedly schematic—as a member of the Nadene linguistic stock.[13] Murdock describes the language:

> Its grammar is characterized, amongst other things, by the extensive use of affixes, the differentiation of active and neutral verbs, and the classification of nouns by shape into such cate-

gories as long, round, and flat.[14]

In this language, Skidegate dialect, "He Who Hunted Birds in His Father's Village" was told. The Haida, "wealthiest of all tribes of the region . . . Vikings of the coast, the scourge of the surrounding tribes," in their rain-swept north Pacific islands, shared in the world-body of oral literature, and recited myths that in appearance at least were sometimes told by Hindu and German peasants.

To relate our version of the Swan-Maiden story to the life of its transmittors, we must next see how the myth mirrors the culture.

3. THE CULTURE IN THE MYTH

This table has been prepared in the same form as Franz Boas' description of the Tsimshian based on their mythology.[15] I have omitted several of his categories, because the larger body of material he is analyzing necessarily contains more aspects of tribal life.

The references are to the abstract of the myth in Chapter I. This table is not intended as complete, but rather as a schematic demonstration of the more obvious culture traits that may be seen in the narrative.

1. Town, Household Goods, and Manufactures.
    The people live in a town in houses (II.1,4). Firewood is gathered by old men. Wooden wedges are used to split the wood (II.9).
    Valuables are kept in nests of boxes (II.4), and salmon eggs are carried in boxes (II.2).
    Twisted cedar branches are used to carry loads with. They may be strengthened with thongs (II.5).
2. Dress and Ornament.
    A chief's son wears two marten-skin blankets (I.1). Hair is cared for with comb and oil (II.3).
3. Fishing, Hunting and Food-gathering.

Salmon are speared in rivers with detachable-point harpoons (II.8). Birds are shot (with bows) (I.2). *Tcal* (I.6), wild-clover roots (I.8), and cranberries (II.4) are gathered.

4. Food.

Prepared by steaming (I.6, II.4). Sometimes people nearly starve (I.8).

5. Travel.

There are trails, upon which people travel by foot (II.2).

6. Social Organization.

There are chiefs (I.1,5) and their families (I.1,5,6), and people (I.8).

7. Family Life.

It is possible to fall in love at first sight, preferring looks to intelligence (I.4). The wife goes to her husband's village (I.5). Marital affection is strong and the husband sorrowful when deserted by his wife (II.1). He is accepted by his wife's people also (II.10). Individuals not in the family group are considered outsiders, as is shown in the statement "She went off as one of a strange family would" (II.9).

8. Festivals.

Marriages are celebrated by a feast, given by the husband's father (I.5).

9. Ethical Concepts and Emotional Life.

Aiding animals and people in distress is rewarding (II.3,4,5). Trickery is acceptable practice in gaining favor (II.8,9). If one is slighted or a social tabu is broken one feels compelled to leave the group in spite of personal preference (II.9).

Sorrow is openly expressed before the group (II.1).

10. Religious and Magical Practices.

Supernatural beings may be propitiated with gifts or aid (II.3,4,5,8,9). With skill one may assume another form by climbing into the creature's skin (I.3,7,9; II.4,6,8).

11. Mythical Concepts.

The world consists of Haida Island (II.5). Somewhere inland a pole reaches to the sky (II.6). One may journey to the sky, but certain knowledge beforehand is useful in discovering the route (II.1,2). The ascent of the pole is perilous, and human bones lie piled around its base (II.6), but in the form of a mouse, rubbing salmon eggs on the pole, one can climb it (II.6). In heaven there is laughing and singing. It is a land with trails and streams. One may see Eagle, Heron, Kingfisher, Black Bear, Grizzly, Loon, Raven, Master Hopper, and the Geese People there (II.7-10).

Loon and Grebe are not strong enough to carry a man back from the sky. Raven is almost strong enough, and carries the man in his armpit (III.1).

Animals are just like people, only living in different skins (II.4,7,9; III.1,2). They can talk (throughout). Animals may have great supernatural power, and be considered "Too great for people even to think of" (II.1) in which case they are supernatural beings, in a class with Master Hopper (II.8), Mouse Woman (II.4) and a woman who carries the mountains of Haida Island (II.5). Supernatural beings sometimes marry with human beings (I.4).

Goose-beings cannot eat human food, but will eat steamed *tcal* (I.6). Grizzly once had no claws, but Eagle gave him some (II.7). Two old men in heaven throw chips into a stream, which become silver salmon (II.9). Being dropped on a reef by Raven turns a man into a seagull. (III.2).

It is clear, from this examination, that even so short a myth as "He Who Hunted Birds in His Father's Village" can contain a wealth of cultural material. There are also rather serious omissions in this myth—particularly concerning the role of the potlatch and prestige valuation. In order to properly evaluate this presentation of cultural content, we shall have to compare the information afforded by the myth with factual material directly pertaining to the Haida.

4. THE CULTURE OF THE HAIDA

Material Culture

When not on hunting, trading, or food-gathering expeditions, the Haida live in "huge rectangular dwellings grouped into villages—usually in a single row facing the beach a few feet above high-water mark."[16] The houses were constructed of upright cedar-post frameworks, with split cedar-plank panels, and split plank roofs, sometimes cut concavely and overlapped like tiles.

> An average house measures about forty feet in depth by thirty in width, with a low roof sloping gently from a height of ten feet at the ridge to six feet at the eaves . . . these substantial houses, the finest in the northwest, will last half a century. . . . The most striking feature of the dwelling is the great "totem pole" which rises from the center of the front or gable end, sometimes to a height of sixty feet. . . .
>
> Entering the door of a large house, one finds on either side of the entrance an inner post, carved and painted, beside which are kept the paddles, weapons, and fishing tackle. To the left, against the front wall of the house, is piled a supply of firewood.[17]

The inside of the house was below ground level, with one or two ledges around the edges, and a fire pit in the center. Boxes, made of folded cedar planks, dishes of carved alder, and bags and baskets of cedar bark or spruce root were placed around the tiers of ledges. Racks of salmon hung over the fire pit.

Clothing was mostly made of woven cedar bark, with skin or fur occasionally worked into the fabric. Both sexes wore waist-length shirts; the men a breechclout, and women a long skirt. A cloak, usually of fur for men and tanned leather for women, was thrown over the shoulder and served as an outer garment. Ceremonial occasions brought forth

> Ceremonial shirts and cloaks with woven or other designs, Chilkat blankets, turbans of shredded cedar bark stained red, and leggings of deerskin ornamented with puffins' beaks which rattle with the movements of the wearer. One of the various types of ceremonial headdresses consists of a tall wooden cylinder, beautifully polished, carved, painted, and inlaid with shells and copper, with a tail of ermine skins behind and a fringe of sea lion whiskers on top. The down of eagles or other birds fills the crown and is scattered like snow in the movements of the dance.[18]

> The women wear their hair long, parted in the middle, and plaited in two braids down the back. The men wear theirs loose and cut off straight just below the shoulders. They also pluck out all facial hairs. Both sexes smear their hair with bear grease scented with aromatic herbs.[19]

Fish were caught with hook and line, dip nets, open mesh baskets, seines and rakes. Salmon were never caught by hook and line, but were netted at stream-mouth, trapped in weirs, or speared with "fish-spears or harpoons with detachable barbed heads of bone."[20] Halibut were caught with hook and line. Occasionally whales were harpooned—a venture requiring trained men, large canoes, and several months of ritual preparation. Deer, elk, and bear were hunted with bow and arrow, sometimes with the aid of dogs. They were also caught in deadfalls or nooses. Birds were trapped, or shot with bows. Women and children gathered

> . . . clams, cockles, mussels, and crabs at ebb tide, and a quantity of birds' eggs in season. They collect and eat a variety of wild roots, herbs, and fruits. They dry certain edible seaweeds and press them into cakes for winter consumption . . . huckleberries, cranberries, salal berries, salmonberries, strawberries, etc. . . . dried and stored, constitute a major item of subsistence.[21]

Although Murdock does not mention wild clover roots, it is interesting to note that "Patches of wild clover root were enclosed in stone fences by the Kwakiutl women, each of whom had her individual plot which she kept weeded to encourage a good growth."[22]

Food was almost always cooked—meat and fish broiled on sticks, or boiled in wooden vessels or watertight baskets with the aid of hot stones. Dried foods were soaked and boiled before eating, or dipped in grease. "The struggle for existence is never severe."[23]

By far the most extensive travelling done by the Haida was in canoe. They made seven types of craft, ranging from flat dugouts to seventy-foot war-and-trading canoes, even the largest carved from a single cedar log. According to Goddard:

> For the most part, the interior of the larger island and the mainland was untraversed by the natives. The greater part of the area is covered by steep and rugged mountains difficult of ascent. The entire area is so heavily forested that travel on foot is extremely difficult. . . . Nearly everywhere the native settlements were on the ocean shore or along navigable rivers.[24]

The skill of Haida craftsmen in woodwork is known all over the world from their totem poles and other ingenious carvings. This skill was also expended on the construction of numerous boxes of all sizes for the storage of food and belongings, and the carving of bowls and dishes, as well as the immense canoes, houses, and totem poles. Certain craftsmen were specialists in their work, and were hired by chiefs or wealthy men for particular jobs. Before the introduction of steel edges by white traders, bone-pointed carving knives, stone-bladed hand adzes, and bone-tipped chisels were the basic tools.

Social Organization

There was no unified government or tribal consciousness among the Haida. The tribe was divided into two exogamous matrilineal moieties, called Ravens and Eagles, the Ravens being most important. "Even the moieties, however, possess no governmental functions; they exist solely for the purpose of regulating marriage and descent. Between them a healthy rivalry prevails, but no hostility."[25] This ranking of moieties, Raven over Eagle, was typical of the Haida method of placing everything on a prestige scale. Even supernatural beings belonged to one or the other moiety.

> Each moiety is subdivided into some twenty matrilineal clans, the fundamental social and political units of the Haidas. A clan is merely a localized segment of a moiety; it consists of that particular branch of a moiety which now inhabits, or at sometime in the past has inhabited, a single village, and it derives its name from that village, not from an animal or the like.[26]

> A clan comprises from one to a dozen separate households, the primary economic units of Haida society. Though a household may number thirty persons or more, it always occupies a single dwelling. . . .

> Authority in the clan and in the household is vested in their respective chiefs. Any man who owns a dwelling, either through inheritance or by amassing sufficient wealth to erect one for himself, is a house chief. He directs the economic activities of his household, protects and cares for its members, exercises a mild paternal authority over them, and is treated with deference. The clan chief is always also a house chief, usually the richest and most powerful in the village.[27]

This only describes two of the social classificatory devices operative among the Haida—kinship and locality. A Haida belongs to the clan of his mother's moiety in whatever locality his parents settled in, usually the woman's village. Rank, however, cuts across local and moiety lines:

> . . . indeed, it may be said that nowhere north of Mexico is the distinction between those of high and those of low birth so sharply drawn as in the West Coast tribes. Three classes of society may be recognized—the nobility, the commoners, and the slaves. . . . High rank is determined primarily by descent

(through the female line). A very important factor, furthermore, in determining rank is wealth, as illustrated more particularly by the distribution of great quantities of property at ceremonial feasts generally known as potlatches.[28]

Marriage outside one's class—between a commoner and a noble—slaves being excluded from any consideration whatsoever—was theoretically impossible. In practice, however, the interaction between wealth and the prestige of nobility made it possible for a commoner to attain a *nouveau-riche* position which, although not improving his class status, made it possible through liberal potlatching for his children to have high status. As Murdock has pointed out[29] status depends on how well one has been potlatched for, not on how well one potlatches. These potlatches imparting status to children were usually part of the house-building or totem-pole raising potlatches, which acted as official naming ceremonies for children as they grew into different age-groups. In this, and its other aspects, the potlatch functioned as the most dynamic integrating institution in the culture. It brought together clans from a wide area, made official the new names of children; the new status of some individual succeeding in the hierarchy of rank to the position of a deceased relative; and provided the opportunity for tribal recitation of songs, tales, and myths—many of the myths associated with clan or individual ownership of a crest, a supernatural animal power regarded as property. The house potlatch, the most spectacular and important of Haida festivals, required property that sometimes took fifteen years to collect. Besides being the occasion of several months of storytelling, dancing, ceremonial acting, and new status announcement, it finally resulted in the group construction of a large new house. This project was climaxed with the ceremonial raising of the totem pole—carved by imported, hired craftsmen—with a slave sometimes placed at the bottom of the hole to be crushed by the weight of the sliding pole as a final sign, on the owner's part, of his utter disdain of wealth. In the light of this and other occasionally destructive acts, we see the Haida goal not to be wealth in itself, but the prestige that can be gained by shaming and overwhelming others by the distribution of it.

On the basis of potlatch-and-wealth competition, an activity which commoners were usually excluded from, the whole range of the nobility was ranked from shiftless "black-sheep" individuals of high descent-status who refused to potlatch, to fabulously wealthy chiefs owning thousands of blankets, valuable coppers, and immense retinues of commoners and slaves.

Wealth, crests, and positions descended in the female line. A chief's successor, in the absence of younger brothers, was his eldest sister's son. A chief's own son—a member of the opposite moiety—received property and position from his maternal uncle. Although property and rank were basic considerations in marriage, particularly among nobility, "Young people of both sexes are permitted considerable freedom before marriage, provided that they belong to opposite moieties."[30] Marriage involved carefully figured exchange of property and eventual establishment of residence with the woman's father, unless he was dead or the groom himself was a house chief.

In spite of the class-structure and rank differentiations, the activities of almost all members of the group, from slave to noble, were essentially the same. Although the chief had prestige, he could not act politically without the consent of his group. The emphasis on wealth led to activity and thrift throughout the tribe, and the combination of a naturally productive environment with an acquisitive society made possible the accumulation of wealth well above the subsistence level.

Religion, Ceremonial Life, Mythology

Our discussion of the potlatch has anticipated the interrelationships between mythology, ceremony, religion, and social organization. As the potlatch enforced and underlined the social organization, so it provided the occasion for the retelling of myths and the reenactment of ceremonies associated with secret societies. Certain myths, being connected with crest traditions and thus property, were bound to be recited, if only to remind the group of the owner's prestige. Songs and art work—carvings and crest designs—were also produced for the occasion.

Haida religion and mythology does not present an ordered cosmology or creation theory. The long cycle of Raven myths accounted for the origin of daylight, water, animals, etc., but without systematization. Raven was a typical trickster type culture hero. The Haida also peopled the world with supernatural beings, the supreme one known as the "Power of the Shining Heavens."

> They believed that human beings had no direct personal relations with this being, who is conceived of as the source from which all the other minor supernatural beings derived their power. It was with these secondary deities that man dealt. . . .
>
> Of the supernatural beings on earth, Creek-women were of great importance. Each stream was believed to have a female divinity whose abode was at the source of the river. She controlled the stream and all the fish in it.
>
> Underneath the Queen Charlotte Islands which constitute the Haida world stood "The sacred one standing and moving." His infrequent movement produced the earthquakes. Thunderbird was responsible for lightning and thunder.[31]

The Haida believed both animals and people had souls, which were essentially the same. The bodies of different animals were merely their "canoes" and all were capable of assuming other forms at will; "or better, they possessed a human form, and assumed their other forms when consorting with men."[32] The killer whales were believed to be the most powerful of all living beings, inhabiting villages under the sea. There were, in this fashion, sea-otter people, salmon people, grizzly people, geese people, etc.

The people of the Northwest Coast believed that animals have souls which are immortal and that they are re-born after death. They are considered practically equals of man in intelligence, and to surpass him in the particulars for which the animal is noted.[33]

These beliefs are basic to Haida mythology, which has as its most typical theme the story of an individual rise to power or wealth through the gaining of supernatural power. An alliance with a supernatural animal or the cultivation of shaman power were the most common means.

In Haida practice, the disciplines of fasting, bathing in cold water, and continence, were undertaken before any extensive hunting or war expeditions. Individuals who were proficient in these practices, experiencing spirit possession while fasting, might become shamans. Shamans were capable of curing, foreseeing the future, and killing by sorcery.

This completes our brief survey of Haida culture. In comparing it with section 3, it may be seen that although several contradictions exist between the culture presented by the myth and that described by ethnographers, in the majority of instances the myth has presented a valid, if limited, picture. The contradictions will be examined in the next section.

5. THE MYTH IN THE CULTURE

To complete our cultural analysis of this myth we must take one more approach: we must study it in terms of what is known of the culture. This section will be an investigation of the cultural meaning of the basic narrative features.

The title, "He Who Hunted Birds in His Father's Village" is to be taken literally in the possessive sense. The village, and the "lake our father owns" of the goose girls are property:

Land, in so far as it is property, belongs to the clan, which enjoys recognized rights to definite hunting grounds, salmon streams, village and camping sites, unusually abundant berry patches, rocky islands where aquatic birds lay their eggs, and strips of beach where whales drift ashore. The chief holds these lands as trustee for the clan, but he can neither sell nor rent them, although in exceptional cases he may alienate them as an indemnity to settle a feud or as a dowry when his daughter marries another chief.[34]

References are to sections of the abstract:

(I.1) He is a chief's son. As such, it is implied that his upbringing has been that of a nobleman, possibly as among the neighboring Tsimshian where

> Children are educated with great care, and particularly the children of chiefs are guarded jealously. Chiefs' sons are taught to be proud of their descent, to be active in acquiring wealth as a means of maintaining their social position, to be lavish in their distribution of food and property, to observe scrupulously all the prescribed taboos, and to refrain from unseemly noise.[35]

Being a male, as a baby he was not of the preferred sex. "The Haidas prefer girl children to boys, since they will add numbers to the clan."[36] As an infant he was treated with the extreme care characteristic of Haida child-training, and nursed for about two years. He was given a potlatch name at birth, one at two years, another at about the age of ten, one at puberty, and perhaps more specialized names, privileges, and crests in his young manhood. Among the privileges attached to his rank is the right of wearing two marten-skin blankets. The importance of privileges, such as this, is not to be underestimated in terms of prestige. They are "Even more important than . . . material possessions."[37] As a chief's son he will not be heir to his father's position, property, or titles. He will inherit his rights and rank from his maternal uncle, who may live in a different village. Thus we see that although the hero is of high rank, his position in the myth is not the same as that of a hero in a European folktale starting "He was the King's son. . ." indicating that he must therefore marry a princess and eventually rule with her over his father's land.

(I.2) In spite of his rank, as an economic unit his activities are little different from those of a commoner or slave. He must contribute by fishing and hunting with the others.

(I.3) As we have seen, there was nothing fantastic in the concept of animals removing their skins and assuming human form to the Haida, but rather it was central to their idea of the animal world.

(I.4) The marriage arrangements commonly expected of noble alliances are completely bypassed here. The fact that the goose girls are of noble birth (evidenced by the statement of their father's ownership of the lake) makes it socially acceptable, and since they are of the goose people, it is not expected that the marriage will follow usual patterns. Numerous Haida myths recount marriages of human beings with supernatural or animal people. "The man who married a killer-whale woman,"[38] "He who married the daughter of the devilfish chief,"[39] are examples of this theme. In none of these are the prescribed courtship customs observed. The preference for the younger sister is understandable, and does not seem to be of particular significance.

(I.5) The marriage feast mentioned is the marriage potlatch, which makes the union socially official. If the chief's son were also heir to control of the tribe, he would probably be dissuaded from forming so unstable an alliance. His particular status in the group makes it possible for him to have both rank and yet act irresponsibly. It is also worthy of note that they take up residence with the husband's father, when matrilocal (at the woman's village) residence is usual among the Haida. This, too, must be explained by the extraordinary nature of marriages between animals and people.

(I.6,7) Although the bride and her mother-in-law are

on familiar terms, mother-in-law avoidance for the male prevails among the Haida. His wife's nightly escapade emphasizes that although she is in human form, she remains a goose at heart.

(I.8) In many Haida myths the theme of starvation appears. Although Murdock believes Haida existence to be easy, a failure of the salmon to run at the expected time, or an extremely heavy winter could make the threat of famine very real to all Northwest Coast Indians. Without a sufficient stock of dried salmon and olachen grease, a tribe could easily starve during the long winter. The superior food-gathering ability of animals, as evidenced in the geese-people's generosity, is an example of the tendency in Haida mythology to credit animals with an easier, better economic life than that of human beings. In many myths individual heroes or whole tribes are saved by the aid of animal people.

(I.9) The apparently inconsequential slight (or breaking of some tabu) that sends the goose wife home is more undestandable in the light of the accentuated social sensitivity of the Haida. Normally, verbal slights, or even such small embarrassing situations as falling down in public, are erased by holding a small potlatch on the spot. A number of blankets are destroyed or given away, and the incident is officially closed. The wife's prestige suffers so much by this slight, that she must leave in spite of her affection for her husband.

(II.1) The nature of the goose woman is clarified by the old man's statement of her supernatural relationship. Although the dividing line between animal-people and supernatural beings is hard to locate, it becomes clear that she falls more readily into the latter class.

(II.2) In preparing for his journey to recover his wife, there is no mention of the ritual purification generally considered necessary before social intercourse with supernatural beings. "The supernatural beings were supposed to be very sensitive to odors."[40] The trail starting "inland behind my house" is mythologically more acceptable in light of the absence of any trails leading into the tangled, mountainous interior—the region where the center of the Haida world is.

(II.3) Lice Man acts as a typical supernatural being in the myth. His sensitivity to being seen by human beings occurs in other Haida myths.

(II.4) Mouse Woman is one of the most recurrent figures in Haida mythology. She almost always appears as a helper to the hero, returning some small kindliness on his part with advice or objects essential to the completion of his venture. The log and hidden-house episode occur in the same basic form in many myths. The nest of boxes is another common Haida myth element.

(II.5) The woman bearing stones is another supernatural being whose good will he must gain before continuing.

(II.6) The pole extending to the sky is accounted for in the Haida myth, "Sacred-one-standing-and-moving, Stone ribs, and Upward,"[41] It appears, in that myth, as holding up the earth. Its occurrence here gives added credulity to this myth and places it, by a device analogous to the learned literary reference, within the canon.

(II.7) The animals mentioned as appearing in heaven to the hero demonstrate the dualistic view of animals as both supernatural, "typical" creatures, and animals as creatures to be hunted. These animals seem to belong in the first category. Their occurrence in the myth might have been associated with certain clan crests, giving it social significance we cannot be completely aware of. The explanatory "how bear came to get his claws" is obviously not essential to the narrative and does not coincide with other Haida traditions about the bear, as far as I know. This too may have some esoteric significance.

(II.8) Half-man, or Master Hopper, is a traditional supernatural being. In the myth, "He-who-got-supernatural-power-from-his-little-finger"[42] he makes an enigmatic appearance in the wonderful house the hero wakes up in:

When day broke he opened his eyes. Something wonderful lay

there into which he awoke. The carvings inside of the house winked their eyes. The carvings on the corner posts of the bedstead moved their tongues at each other. In a rear corner of the house something stood making a noise. That was Greatest Hopper, they say.

The activity of Master Hopper in the Swan-Maiden myth is more intelligible when it is remembered that salmon are the staple food of the Haida. The needs and pursuits of even the supernatural beings in the sky are the same as those of the Haida.

(II.9) This is also demonstrated in the work of the two old men, who create salmon. As far as I know, this is not a common tradition for the origin of salmon, but rather an example of one of the many ways creatures can be made.

(II.10) The hero is at last in the home of his wife's father. According to Haida custom, as we have seen, he should have been here to begin with. In the mythology, however, it is usual for supernatural fathers-in-law to subject their daughters' human husbands to a number of dangerous tests which must be overcome by the exercise of corresponding supernatural power. The incidents taking place in the hero's journey to his wife's home apparently take the place of tests in this myth. It is significant to note that among the Haida "A man shows great deference in the presence of the male relatives of his wife."[43]

(III.1) His dislike of his wife's home is also thematic in Haida literature in supernatural-marriage tales. Although by rights he should be content in his wife's village, the mythological hero is seldom satisfied with his wife's people. Raven is, of course, a traditional figure in all Northwest Coast mythology. He is seen here not as the culture-hero individual Raven, but as the typical Raven (again distinct from the animal Raven). Even as typical Raven, he is very strong, and carries the hero in a traditional place—his armpit. Heroes are often hidden or carried this way by supernatural beings. A brave social evolutionist might argue that the absence of the customary matrilocal residence in this myth is indicative of an internal trend among the Haida away from their matrilineal society, and towards the patrilineal stage. If one accepted this, implausible as it is, it might help in part to explain the knotty problem of

(III.2) the end of the hero. With the social evolutionist we might argue that although matrilocal residence has been rejected, the hero (and patrilineal principle) are in a stage of change and not yet ready to be assimilated by the total culture. Thus the hero is declassed in this myth, being unable to live with his wife, and having no status to return to in his own village. Becoming a seagull is perhaps the simplest solution. The fact is, however, that unless one simply accepts the fact that Raven was tired, and that when human beings are dropped on reefs they turn into seagulls, the conclusion of this myth is puzzling—even in terms of Haida culture.

When something happens in a myth or tale which cannot be explained by cultural study or in terms of narrative necessity, the next step would be to look at the variants of the tale in neighboring cultures to see how that situation has been handled elsewhere. Doing this is tacitly admitting that the myth is the product of historical processes of invention, borrowing, diffusion, and survival, as well as the reflection of a way of life. It was shown in section 2 of this chapter how all of Northwest Coast culture shares certain basic traits. Clearly there has been interaction in many phases of culture among the tribes of the area, and the northwest, in its turn, has been subject to influence from all of North America and perhaps northeastern Asia.

We shall now extend our comparative scope to include the world, seeing the myth not as the isolated product of a small group, but as a unique patterning of elements common to folk literature almost everywhere.

In this chapter, it has been seen how the culture and myth reflect each other. This myth, although not expressing the most central Haida ideals of competition, wealth, and prestige, nonetheless can be seen on the simplest level as a mythical *divertissement*, an adventure story of a chief's son. Although some folkways are played rather freely with, the myth deviates in no serious way from the actual conditions of Haida culture, and at most points is in complete accord with it.

CHAPTER III

VERSIONS OF THE MYTH

1. THE METHOD

In order to know what in the Swan-Maiden myth is uniquely Haida, and what components transcend linguistic and cultural barriers, one must study and compare the historically
related versions. Comparison is based on the identity of
the underlying narrative pattern, designated "type" in modern folklore study, and smaller units called "motifs" which
have logical similarity. Stith Thompson best defines the distinction between type and motif:

> A type is a traditional tale that has an independent existence.
> It may be told as a complete narrative and does not depend for
> its meaning on any other tale. It may indeed happen to be told
> with another tale, but the fact that it may appear alone attests
> its independence. It may consist of only one motif or many.
> Most animal tales and jokes and anecdotes are types of one mo-
> tif. The ordinary *Märchen* (tales like Cinderella or Snow White)
> are types consisting of many of them.

A motif is the smallest element in a tale having power to persist in tradition. In order to have this power it must have something unusual and striking about it. Most motifs fall into three classes. First are the actors in a tale—gods, or unusual animals, or marvelous creatures like witches, ogres, or fairies, or even conventionalized human characters like the favorite youngest child or the cruel stepmother. Second come certain items in the background of the action—magic objects, unusual customs, strange beliefs, and the like. In the third place there are single incidents—and these comprise the great majority of motifs. It is this last class that can have an independent existence and may therefore serve as true tale-types. By far the largest number of traditional types consist of these single motifs. . . . A type-index implies that all versions of a type have a genetic relationship; a motif-index makes no such assumption.[1]

Boas has noted the importance of distinguishing between the two lines of inquiry possible in the comparative study of a myth: "—the one, the investigation into the history of tales; the other, the investigation of the origin of traditions or ideas common to many or all mythologies."[2] In this chapter, the prime consideration will be the history of the tale, that is, the type. The motifs, which have independent transmission occasionally, are closer in nature to the "ideas common to all mythologies," and will be mainly studied as they occur within the type, although independent occurrence of certain motifs will be noted. "Historical study," in the sense used here, does not mean explication of chronological development, or search for ultimate origins, but rather the correlations of geographical distribution with the different versions of demonstrably historically related myths and tales. For the majority of tales, it will never be possible to know the place of origin, owing to the immense time-depth and complexity of oral literature. Knowledge of origins, at present, is not even considered as valuable as the understanding of processes in diffusion and adaptation.

Certain criteria must be established between unrelated but logically similar types and motifs, and those historically related as well. The dissemination of tales, giving rise to different but related versions, has followed two basic processes: first, via the migration of a group to a new area, bearing its literature with.it, which becomes changed in time as the whole culture changes. Second, a tale passes from one group to another, being translated into the new language. Bilingual individuals living at cultural boundaries or mixed marriages are often responsible for the translation of a myth or tale, and the new group then gradually alters the tale to fit into its existing body of oral literature.

Variations of these two processes are possible: as for instance an isolated individual bearing a tale over a long distance, becoming accepted into a new culture and learning the language—consequently adding his tale to the literature of the group. These exceptional means of transmission are probably unimportant to any extensive diffusion of folk literature. Furthermore, it is impossible to know the history of migrations of most primitive peoples, and often neighboring culture areas fail to share basic tales which have been transmitted by a roundabout route, to geographically more distant groups. Attempts at defining historic relationships in mythology by the geographical movements of the peoples involved are thus unreliable, if at all possible.

The working rules for establishing identity between tales were formulated by Boas:

> First, the tale or formula the distribution of which is investigated, and is to be explained as due to historical contact, must be so complex, that an independent origin of the sequence of non-related elements seems to be improbable. . . .
> The second rule is, that for a satisfactory proof of dissemination, continuous distribution is required.[3]

To present the total distribution of the Swan-Maiden myth would require the endless citing of versions and variants filed in folklore archives all over the world. This comparative study can be only the barest presentation of available Swan-Maiden material. I shall first show related Northwest Coast versions, then cite total American distribution, and establish the identity of American variants. The relationship between northeast Asian folklore and that of the Northwest Coast of America will be shown. A capsule outline of the world distribution of both motifs and the type, based on Stith Thompson's Motif-Index[4] and Antti Aarne's "The Types of the Folktale,"[5] will be followed by a general commentary on the Swan-Maiden type in Europe and Asia and some example of the tale's incorporation into conscious written literary genres.

2. THE MYTH IN NORTH AMERICA

First, the basic narrative action of the myth must be established, to provide a basis for comparison with other versions. Although the term "Swan Maiden" has served as a convenient catchword in describing this tale so far, it will be seen that the swan-maiden episode is only one motif within the type pattern, and may be substituted for without destroying the type identity. "He Who Hunted Birds in His Father's Village" in it most compressed form:

1. Man wins supernatural maiden for wife.
2. She is insulted, and leaves.
3. Man goes on quest for her.
4. They are reunited.
5. He wishes to return to his home. He is transformed into a bird.

In the Northwest Coast culture area, there are few myths containing the bathing goose-girl episode (I.3,4) aside from the Haida, although the marriage of men to animals or supernatural beings is a very common theme. Boas briefly notes it as "a plot underlying miscellaneous stories."[6] Two Tlingit myths recorded by Swanton[7] may be safely identified with the Haida version, sharing as they do the complex type pattern utilizing several motifs. The two Tlingit versions concern men who marry Brant Women (Brant is a species of goose, *Branta nigricans*). The bathing-and-skin episode is repeated in the first myth (no. 24), and in both myths the pattern of winning, losing, and regaining the wife occur. In no. 24 the man stays with the Brant and becomes one of them in physical form; in the second (no. 54) the man is finally abandoned by his wife's tribe on a rock at sea and carried back to his own village by the *gusyaduli* bird, who prohibits him to open his eyes during flight. He returns safely. It is conceivable that the tabu against looking ing during flight—a rather common prohibition in similar situations of Indian mythology—was at one time a condition of Raven's carrying the hero from the upper world in the Haida version. If so, then the hero's transformation into a seagull would be the consequence of breaking the tabu, and the apparent illogicallity of the Haida version is due only to the faulty memory of an informant.

The half-man (II.8) is also common to Northwest Coast folklore. It often occurs independent of the Swan-Maiden tale:

> Persons who consist of one side of a body only, occur in quite a number of tales.
>
> In the Tlingit story of the four brothers it is said that the brothers reach the end of the world, where they meet a large man with but one leg, who is spearing salmon. When he is through, he puts the salmon on two strings, which he carries in his mouth. Then follows the story of the theft of the salmon-harpoon. . . .
>
> The Bellacoola tell of a man called Qasana who consists of only one side of the body and who marries a wife carved of wood. The Chippewayan also tell of a monster of a similar kind.[8]

For the stolen harpoon episode,

> Fifteen versions have been recorded . . . The essential contents of the story refer to a fisherman who owns a valuable harpoon, which is taken away by a Transformer who assumes the shape of a fish, allows himself to be harpooned, and breaks the

harpoon line. Later on he assumes human shape, and returns the harpoon-line to the fisherman.[9]

Twenty versions have been recorded of the wood-splitting slave episode, which Boas identifies with the two old men splitting wood (II.9). The wood-splitting slave usually appears at a crucial point in the quest of the hero, and either voluntarily or for some favor aids him. In some versions he acts as gatekeeper to the wife's otherworld village, and is silenced with tobacco much like Cerberus is thrown cakes in Greek mythology.[10]

A number of common Northwest Coast motifs converge in the Haida myth. The Swan-Maiden marriage motif, the identification of half-man with the stolen harpoon episode and the placement of these motifs within the otherworld journey motif, and Raven's appearance at the end, make the Haida Swan-Maiden myth very compressed and rich in symbolic significance within the corpus of Northwest mythology.

The dissemination of tales and myths in North America is not to be considered limited to culture areas. Boas argues that "diffusion of tales was just as frequent and just as widespread in America as it has been in the Old World."[11]

In his comparative study of the Swan-Maiden tale in North America, Thompson cites references to versions found in the following groups: Greenland, Baffin Land, Point Barrow, Cumberland Sound, and Kodiak Eskimo; Tlingit, Haida, Wishosk, Ute, Uintah, Wichita, Fox, Micmac, Passamaquoddy, and Huron-Wyandot Indians.[12] This indicates distribution across the whole length of North America. Boas' dictum of geographical continuity in versions is established by way of the Eskimo:

> . . . diffusion of tales between the Eskimo and the Indian tribes of the western half of our continent has been quite exclusive. On the other hand, notwithstanding many assertions to the contrary, there are hardly any close relations between the tales of the Algonquin and the Eskimo . . . I found one or possibly

two elements that belong to Eskimo lore—the capture of a bathing girl by taking away her clothing . . .[13]

Other versions are the result of borrowing from early Europeans, particularly French-Canadians. Thus there are two levels of Swan-Maiden mythology in North America: one pre-Columbian—Haida, Eskimo, and Algonquin among these in this category; and recent tales borrowed from European oral literature. These borrowings took place in Eastern American cultures. Quite possibly, the European versions were often merged with pre-Columbian versions already in the mythology.

If "Supernatural or animal wife" is substituted for the more specific "Swan-Maiden" episode of the Haida myth, an immense number of Indian tales are seen to parallel the type. Motifs from other tales also occur in some versions, notably the "Cindarella" theme (a despised person wins respect and power with supernatural aid) and the "Mysterious Housekeeper" episode, in which a man discovers a supernatural woman keeping house for him secretly, marries her, breaks a tabu she has put upon him, and consequently loses her. An example of convergence of several types in one tale is the Cree "Mudjikiwis"—remotely related to Longfellow's poem.

> Ten brothers, the eldest of them being named Mudjikiwis, keep house together. When they return from the hunt they find that their house has been mysteriously put in order. They take turns in remaining home to investigate the mystery. One of the brothers succeeds in finding a girl who has been hiding from them. He marries her, and she remains as housekeeper for the brothers. Mudjikiwis, the eldest brother, becomes jealous and tries to win the girl from his brother. When she rejects him he shoots her, and goes back home. When her husband misses her and follows her, she tells him that she is supernatural and that after four days if he will come for her, he can find her. He becomes impatient and comes for her on the third day. She therefore disappears, leaving bloody tracks behind her. Her husband now undertakes a long quest to recover her.

It is from this point that the tale follows very closely the European story of the lost Swan Maiden.

> He encounters a mysterious old woman helper, who has an inexhaustible meat pot the size of a thimble. She informs him that his wife is one of ten daughters of the supernatural people of the sky. From this old woman he is sent in turn to three others, each older than the last. They give him magic objects to help him climb to the upper world. By means of these objects, and by the power of transformation which they give him, he succeeds in overcoming all the perils of the journey and reaching the upper world. He finds there is to be a contest to see who is going to marry his wife. He wins the contest, and takes back not only his own wife, but her nine sisters for his nine brothers.
>
> If this is actually an aboriginal tale, it is one of the most elaborately developed of any thus far reported. But the combination of the lost supernatural wife, the difficult quest for her, the succession of old woman helpers, the climbing of a slippery mountain into the upper world, the arrival there just as the wife is about to marry another—all these are so close to the Swan Maiden tale that we surely have at least a considerable amount of contamination.[14]

The Swan-Maiden myth also occurs in South America, but it is very difficult to tell if the versions are the result of European borrowing, or an early dissemination from North America. The Arawak Indians of Guiana tell a very complex version: A beautiful royal vulture, daughter of Anuanima, sovereign of a race whose country is above the sky, is captured by a hunter. She falls in love with him, and takes off her feathers, revealing herself as a beautiful girl. He goes to live with her in the sky, and all goes well until he expresses a wish to visit his mother. They immediately discard him, and set him on the top of a high tree covered with prickles. The spiders spin cords, the fluttering birds ease his descent, and he reaches the ground in safety. Then follow many years of attempting to regain his wife, and only by great strength and skill does he escape attempts to destroy him. At last he gets the birds on his side, and they bear him as commander above the sky. He is slain in battle by a young warrior who turns out to be his own son, born after his expulsion from the sky and brought up in ignorance of his father. The legend ends with the conflagration of the house of the royal vultures, who, hemmed in by crowds of hostile birds, are unable to use their wings, and are forced to fight and die in their human forms.[15]

The Haida myth is thus related to a large number of widely distributed American Indian tales, and it parallels an even larger number of tales with the supernatural wife loss-of-wife quest-for-wife pattern. Some variants may have had historical contact with the European Swan Maiden, others not. It is clear that the Haida myth as outlined here is conceptually and historically significant to all of North American mythology.

3. FROM AMERICA TO ASIA

Swan-Maiden myths have been transmitted to all parts of Eurasia. They have traveled freely through all of North America. To prove the historical connection between the Haida myth and Old World folk literature, the connection between northeast Asia and the Northwest Coast cultures of America must be shown. Many traits in material culture are shared. One of the most significant is the use of slat-armor—

> . . . consisting of cuirasses and other protective devices made of rods or slats, of wood, bone, or ivory, securely lashed together. If this type of armor should have developed from Chinese and Japanese patterns it would be proof of long-continued cultural influence that extended northward and south-eastward.

> Attention might also be called to the peculiar use of wood-shavings, grasses, and shredded bark as religious symbols which characterize the ceremonials of the Ainu, Koryak, Chukchee,

and of the coast tribes of British Columbia and southern Alaska.

Considering these phenomena the modern transfer of culture elements from Siberia to America does not seem suprising, and does not necessitate the assumption of very great antiquity of this connection.[16]

The folklore of northeast Asia and northwestern America has been extensively studied by Gudmund Hatt, who concludes that the Eurasian and American Swan-Maiden tales are historically related:

Regarding the geographical distribution, it should be observed . . . that the motif is found among the Chukchees and, in similar forms, among the Eskimos, as mentioned by Bogoras. The connection between the Old and the New World is therefore unbroken. It should also be observed, that the swan-maiden motif is old as well in China as in Japan. If it is denied that a part of the swan-maiden versions in America are due to transmissions from Asia, one may as well doubt that the continuous distribution of this motif in other parts of the world can be regarded as the result of diffusion.

In Oceania, the swan-maiden motif is very common in Indonesia, Melanesia, and Australia. . . . The motif has reached America by the northern way, over North East Asia. A transmission via Polynesia is unlikely.[17]

The Kolyma, a northeastern Asiatic Tungus tribe, have this version: Three girls, when they go berry-picking, put on goose skins and fly to the berry patch, discard their skins to pick berries, and fly home again in the evening. One day half-man (One-side) steals the wings of the youngest and she agrees to marry him. She has a son by him. The other two sisters come while One-side is hunting and carry the wife and child away. As they fly, One-side shoots off the little finger of the boy with an arrow. He seeks his wife through many villages, and one day sees a mistreated little boy in one. He identifies him by the missing finger as his son, kills his wife's cruel brothers and sisters, and reveals himself as a two-sided, handsome young man.[18]

In this myth the winning, loss, and regaining of the wife is contained intact; but even similar motifs—such as half-man, and the quest for the wife—are handled differently. This version is an example of the Siberian myths which stand between the more sophisticated Chinese and European versions and the distinctly American tales.

4. THE MYTH THROUGHOUT THE WORLD

Having secured the validity of historical connection between American and Old World Swan-Maiden tales, it is possible to utilize comparative folklore scholarship dealing with European and Asiatic material with assurance of its relation to the Haida myth. So far, I have been tentatively exploring the nature and distribution of the type as defined by the Haida version. Since it is clear that the narrative action of the Haida myth is paralleled in many other tales, I will now start with the type as defined by comparative study, and present the Haida version within the framework of a type and motif breakdown based on world comparisons, to see how closely it approximates the world-type, and to uncover the distribution of the motifs. Aarne's *Type-Index*[19] and Thompson's *Motif-Index*[20] are the basis of this study. Aarne's book, as enlarged by Thompson, is divided into Animal Tales, Ordinary Folktales, and Jokes and Anecdotes. It is numbered from 1 to 2499, each number representing an independent tale falling into a specific category; for example numbers 400-459 are tales of "Supernatural or enchanted husband (wife) or other relatives." The analysis of each type is broken down into the basic episodes, and within each episode the more common variations are noted. Appended to each type analysis is an outline of the areal distribution and references to important collections and studies of the type. *The Motif-Index* is a six volume work following the same general form, but without historical concern:

> The *Motif-Index* . . . attempts to bring together material from everywhere and arrange it by a logical system. It makes no assumption that items listed next to each other have any genetic relationship, but only that they belong in neighboring logical categories. The classification is for the practical purpose of arranging and assorting narrative material so that it may be easily found. . . .
>
> A numbering system was devised, remotely similar to that used by the Library of Congress, so that the Index can be indefinitely expanded at any point. Every motif has a number indicating its place in the classification. Chapters (indicated by capital letters) are divided into large groups, usually of 100 numbers, and these in turn into tens, etc.[21]

The chapter headings designate the following content: A.—Mythological motifs, B.—Animals, C.—Tabu, D.—Magic, E.—The Dead, F.—Marvels, G.—Ogres, H.—Tests, J.—The Wise and the Foolish, K.—Deceptions, L.—Reversal of Fortune, M.—Ordaining the Future, N.—Chance and Fate, P.—Society, Q.—Rewards and Punishments, R.—Captives and Fugitives, S.—Unnatural Cruelty, T.—Sex, V.—Religion, W.—Traits of Character, X.—Humor, Z.—Miscellaneous. Bibliographical references according to geographical area are included in the classifications of the more basic motifs.

Although the mechanics of this classification may seem unnecessarily complex when applied to such a small myth as the Haida Swan Maiden, it is the only way possible to show how much of the total content of the Haida version is composed of elements not only reflecting the culture, but part of the basic material in folk literature everywhere. The excerpted passages are direct quotations from Aarne's *Type-Index*; the text following each quotation from Aarne deals with the parallel episode in the Haida version—designated by the abstract number at the beginning of each paragraph, and broken down into motifs as classified by Thompson:

Type 400. The man on a Quest for his Lost Wife.

Magic objects or animals as helpers (as introduction frequently the Swan Maiden).

I. *The Hero.* (a) A father unwittingly promises his son to a sea monster (giant etc.). (b) The boy is adopted by a king. (c) The ogre wants to take the boy but cannot since he has a bible under his arm (See Mt 810).[22] (d) A field is tramped down; the brothers keep watch but only the youngest remains by his post. (e) A prince is on a hunt.

(I,1,2) The Haida hero is seen as motif H 1222, *Prince a-hunting enters on quest.* (Aarne I.e).

II. *The Enchanted Princess.* (a) The hero goes in a self-moving boat to foreign land or castle or (b) the hero and another find a bewitched princess in the castle. (c) They are rescued by the hero's enduring in silence three frightful nights in the castle or (d) by his sleeping by the princess three nights without looking at her or disturbing her. (e) Girls in swan coats: the hero steals one coat and will give it back to the owner only if she will marry him. (f) The hero marries the princess.

(I.3)—Motif D 361.1. *Swan Maiden* (Aarne II.e). A swan transforms herself at will into a maiden. She resumes her swan form by putting on her swan coat. (It is difficult to tell in most Swan-Maiden tales whether the primary form is swan or maiden: the incident may belong to D 161.1—transformation person to swan.) Found in types 313 "The girl as helper in the hero's flight," 400 "The man on a quest for his lost wife"; and 465A "The man persecuted because of his beautiful wife, the quest for the Unknown." This motif is found in Spanish, Germanic, French, Arabian, Persian, Ceylon, Japanese, Indonesian, Polynesian-Melanesian, Australian, Siberian, and North American Indian collections.

(I.4) B 653.1 *Marriage to Swan Maiden.* (Aarne II.f). Related to motif F 302.4.2, "Fairy comes into man's power when he steals her wings," and K 1335, "Seduction (or wooing) of bathing girl by stealing her clothes." These motifs are usually distributed in conjunction with D 361.1.

III. *His visit Home.* (a) The hero wants to go home on a visit. (b) The princess gives him a wishing ring or (c) three wishes. (d) She forbids him: to call for her to come to him, or (e) to utter her name, or (f) to sleep, (g) to eat or (h) to drink. (i) She has promised to meet the hero, but an enemy by means of a magic pin makes him sleep when she comes.

This episode is missing in the Haida version.

IV. *Loss of the Wife.* (a) He calls upon her to come so as to show how beautiful she is or (b) breaks one of the other prohibitions. (c) She comes, takes the ring and disappears and gives him iron shoes which he must wear out before he finds her again. (d) The swan maiden (see II.e) finds her swan coat and flies away.

(I.9) C 31 Tabu: *offending supernatural wife.* Upon slight offense the wife leaves for her old home. Thompson cites English, North American Indian, and Maori sources. This motif is related to C 952—"Immediate return to other world because of broken tabu," which is listed for Greek (Persephone and Thetis) and Congo occurrence. Her return is accomplished by motif D 531, "Transformation by putting on skin," a motif cited for Irish, English, North American Indian, Jamaica, North Carolina Negro, and Surinam sources. Compare Aarne IV.d.

V. *The Search.* (a) He sets out in search of her and (b) meets people who rule over wild animals, birds, and fish. (c) An old eagle gives him advice. He asks his way of the sun and moon who know nothing, (b) but the wind shows him his way. (f) Three old women help him; (g) he must climb up a steep mountain without looking back. (h) He meets people who are fighting over magic objects and gets the objects in a trick trade; e.g. saddle, hat, mantle, boots, sword.

(II.1-9) This section may be studied under the general motif H 1385.3, *Quest for vanished wife.* (Aarne V.a). Thompson lists Hindu, Oceanic (New Zealand, Mangaia, Nieue, Chatham Island, Hawaii, New Britain, Admiralty Islands, New Hebrides) and Indonesian collections. Within the framework of the quest, the following motifs occur:

(II.1,2) N 825.2. *Old man as helper.* This motif is listed as found in Seneca and Kaffir sources. A related motif is D 621, "Magic objects received from old man."

(II.3) Motif N 810, *Supernatural helpers* as a very general heading includes Lice Man, who must himself be listed under F 500, "Remarkable person" although no specific reference to him is to be found in the *Motif Index.* As the hero progresses to the next helper, the motif H 1235, "Succession of helpers on quest" is recognizable. Thompson cites Italian and North American Indian sources in relation to it.

(II.4) Mouse Woman is another supernatural helper. As she appears in both mouse and human form, she may be related to several motifs. B 431.2, "Helpful mouse," is cited for Kaffir and Basuto sources, but these are apparently literal mice. Motif B 320, "Reward of helpful animal" is related in this instance to Q 140, "Miraculous or magic reward" which in our myth is D 812, "Magic object received from a supernatural being." The magic object is the mouse skin which functions as motif D 1330, "Magic object works physical change"—the transformation of man to mouse, motif D 117.1.

(II.5) The woman carrying the "mountains of the Haida Island" has been assigned a task which is probably best classified under H 1130, "Superhuman tasks." The hero's action falls under the heading Q 40, "Kindness rewarded." The reward is advice as to the route of his quest.

(II.6) From here on, the quest of the hero for his wife may be subclassified under motif H 1260, *Quest to the upper world.* The motifs included under the heading, "Otherworld Journeys" (F 0-199) are distributed all over the globe, and are often found in conjunction with a quest motif. The pole reaching the sky, motif A 665.2 "Pillar supporting sky" is cited for a Siberian source by Thompson. For the Haida the pole, held by the supernatural being "Sacred-one-standing-and-moving" was also the support of Haida Island—extending from the upper world through the earth, and supported from below—motif A 843, "Earth supported on a post." Thompson notes Finno-Ugric, Tlingit, and Hare sources for this motif, commenting that the post has an old woman as guardian, who shakes the pole when hungry, causing earthquakes. It will be recalled that the Haida deity's "infrequent movement produced the earthquakes."[23] As a means of access to the upper world, the pole may be classified as F 58, "Tower (column) to upper world." The heap of bones at its base indicates that motif F 151.1, "Perilous path to otherword" is also relevant. North American Indian sources are noted for this motif.

(II.7) In the otherworld, the hero sees a stream (F 162.2, "Rivers in the otherworld") and then animals—motif F 167.1, "Animals in the otherworld." Bear speaks to eagle (B 211, "Animal uses human speech," Hindu and French Canadian sources) and asks him for his claws: motif A 2240, "Animal characteristics: obtaining another's qualities."

(II.8) Master Hopper, or half-man, has already been seen as a widely distributed mythical character. He is classified as F 525, *Person with half a body.* Ostiak, Votiak, Chinese, North American Indian, Basuto, Zulu, and Indonesian sources are listed. The transformation of man to salmon is motif D 176, listed for a Norse source. Although the text of the Haida version is not clear in this respect, the hero's exchange of his own spearpoint for Master Hopper's is to be related to D 831, "Magic object acquired by trick exchange." (Aarne V.h).

> VI. *The Recovery.* (a) He meets the north wind and (b) by means of his magic objects reaches the castle where the princess is about to be married. (c) The new bridegroom is killed. (d) Recognition by ring in cake.—(e) Sometimes followed by tasks to be performed and transformation flight.

(II.9) The two old men provide the hero with the last essential knowledge, playing, as we have seen, something of the role of doorkeepers. (A 671.1).

(II.10) The hero and his wife are reunited.

(III.1,2) Return from the upperworld by means of a bird is classified as F 62, *Birds carry person from upper world*. Comparison of the Haida hero's return with Aarne's VI.2—tasks to be performed and transformation flight—indicates that the Haida myth may have lost the ogre character of the wife's father in transmission, while retaining the transformation flight episode, then neglecting to retransform the hero back to human form because of the nature of his departure. Transformation to seagull is classified as D 154. Under the general heading, "Transformation man to bird," Irish, Norse, Greek, Finnish, Maori, and Thompson Indian collections are listed.

5. CONCLUSION

In the comparative study it is seen that many motifs common to all of world literature have been employed in the Haida myth, without violence being done to either the essential narrative, or the cultural content. The amazing flexibility and vitality of the type form is partially responsible for the myth's adaptability. Thompson writes,

> With all the many variations in the earlier part of the story, and with the wealth of detail possible in the central action, it is remarkable that the tale should retain a definite enough quality to be considered a real entity. And yet the characteristic incidents of the quest are so constant that it is not difficult to recognize this tale type in spite of the almost kaleidoscopic variations it has assumed. Three stories of Grimm's famous collection (Nos. 92, 93, and 193) deal with this material, each handling it in a different fashion. Sometimes it appears as part of a local legend, and sometimes it has received elaborate literary treatment.[24]

Literary versions range from the tale of "The Hasan of Bassorah" [25] in the Arabian Nights to the "Volundarkvitha" poem of the Eddas.[26] From Teutonic and Celtic sources, Swan-Maiden motifs went into medieval romance, notably the "Knight of the Swan" series:

> The oldest literary version is found in the Dolopathos (ed. Hilka, 1913, p. 80, ff), which was written about 1190 by Johannes de Alta Silva . . . all of the characters are unnamed; the mother is a *nympha* whom a young lord finds bathing in a fountain, takes home, and marries. She is clearly a swan maiden. . . .[27]

Her son becomes the Knight of the Swan. In later versions his Swan-Maiden origin is obscured, but he retains a supernatural nature:

> In other versions the knight is ancestor of Godfrey of Bouill-grin, son of Percival, the tale being thus linked to Arthurian romance. The Swan-knight who comes and goes so mysteriously is a denizen of the Other World and his disappearance was the result of his wife's asking his name or whence he had come.[28]

At the other end of the Eurasian landmass, the Swan-Maiden tale has been transformed into a Japanese Noh play, "The Robe of Feathers," *Hagoromo*, by Seami.

> The story is a version of the tale of the Swan Maiden so well known in the folk-lore of various nations . . . in its idealized version in the Noh drama, the maiden is represented as one of the fairies in attendance on the heavenly princes who reside in the Moon palace, an idea clearly taken from a Buddhist story of the moon. Moreover, in this version the maiden preserves her virginity intact and chief motive of the tale is the contrast between the noble purity of the celestial maiden and the greed of mankind.[29]

The seventeenth-century Chinese writer Pu Sung-ling retold the tale in his *Strange Stories from a Chinese Studio* as "A Supernatural Wife." [30]

The wide distribution of the Swan-Maiden myth, combined with the extensive occurrence of supernatural wife or husband tales, has led some writers to consider all supernatural marriage myths as ultimately identical. Hartland states that:

> The one idea running through them all is that of a man wedding a supernatural maiden and unable to retain her; and if he desire to recover he must pursue her thither and conquer his right to her by undergoing superhuman penance or performing superhuman tasks.[31]

"Cupid and Psyche," "Peleus and Thetis," "Beauty and the Beast," and the Scottish ballad "The Great Silkie o' Sule Skerrie" are thus to be considered as aspects of the same complex of mythological ideas and narrative. Although there is obvious logical similarity between these narratives, it is unlikely that they could all be shown to be historically related. The mythological structures which can be abstracted from various tales and myths are independently invented, or disseminated over long distances across language, race, and culture boundaries, all the while retaining structural identity. The most recurrent ones are relatively few in number and are "preferably attached to animals, celestial bodies, and other personified phenomena of nature."[32] They all show the vitality and flexibility of the Swan-Maiden myth in oral tradition.

An understanding of the relationship between cultural and comparative aspects of a myth on any level but similarity-or-difference, and insight into psychological factors behind the history of a myth, calls for the other side of comparative study—the investigation of "traditions and ideas common to many or all mythologies." The next chapter will undertake this investigation, in hope of discovering the social or psychological basis for the Swan-Maiden tale's long popularity.

CHAPTER IV

S O U R C E S   O F   T H E   M Y T H

1. METHODS

In trying to fathom the reasons for the frequency of certain
mythological motifs and forms, one is confronted with an
absence of any organized scholarship working with similar
assumptions toward an agreed goal. In this chapter we leave
the realms of respectable cultural and comparative folklore.
The purified and cautious students of Boas and the folklorists utilizing methods of the Finnish scholars and Stith
Thompson consider any attempt to establish "basic causes"
and "ultimate sources" risky business.

   The approach of this chapter cannot be justified in
terms of current critical method. Nonetheless, establishing
multilevel significance in a myth requires that we search
through scientifically unsound, and contradictory, outmod-
ed, or suspicious theories. My reliance on these theories
will be so slight as to permit no real exposition of any of
them, but wherever they have extended into Swan-Maiden

mythology with some possibility of truth, I have attempted to fit them into a pattern which is significant in terms of the myth itself. In the course of the argument the more glaring difficulties and misconceptions will be described. Stith Thompson states his attitude toward Swan-Maiden theories of the past:

> A re-examination of all the material relating to this story is necessary before any conclusions as to its history can be reached. Many of the things written about it in the past are clearly antiquated. Some of these studies fail to distinguish between this tale and others of supernatural and offended wives, such as the legend of Melusine. Others interest themselves in the situation because it seems to have some relation to primitive totemism or to a primitive matriarchy. It is, of course, possible that some such ideas lie behind the motifs in this story. But these older investigators were purely theoretical and unrealistic in their approach. They did not actually attempt to answer the question as to just when and just how this particular tale was composed and in just what manner it has been propagated.[1]

> A century ago these scholars were talking with the utmost certainty and dogmatism of these supernatural spouses, telling us that they represented now this, now that phenomenon of sky or cloud or seasonal change. A generation later these creatures were dogmatically described as always essentially animals and as related to primitive totemistic ideas. Still later the ritualistic school had its inning and all these stories became embodiments of ancient rites. And even today there remain some scholars who assert that they have the key that unlocks this mystery. This key they find in the interpretation of dreams.[2]

The solar theories may well be ignored, but totemism, ritual, and dream theories—and some very recent blendings of all three—will be applied to the Swan-Maiden tale. The study will progress from an outline of underlying social customs connected with the myth on the basis of social-evolutionist assumptions, to a theoretical location of the souce of the myth motifs geographically and historically. The major objections to the theoretical principles required in these methods will be briefly stated, followed by a linkage of motifs with mental characteristics, and the total quest-myth pattern will be presented as psychological-metaphysical truth in symbolic form.

2. THE MYTH AND SOCIAL BEHAVIOR

The social behavior implied here relates specifically to beliefs and institutions referred to as supernaturalism, totemism, tabu, magic, religion, and ritual. The distinctions between these phenomena are often difficult to make, and it is seldom possible to find universally accepted definitions for any of them. They may be roughly related to the Swan-Maiden myth in the following order:

> Hero—often of divine birth—supernaturalism
> Supernatural marriage with animal or supernatural
>   being—supernaturalism and totemism.
> Loss-of-wife—breaking of tabu
> Quest for wife—magic, tabu, supernatural cosmogony.

These appear as principles of action within the narrative. The principles fit into certain widespread religious and social configurations from which, it is argued, the narrative derives its source and meaning. The referent of myth as symbol is in this view not nature (the fact that swans and maidens are interchangeable in the myth proves nothing about real animals and people), but types of social customs. The Swan Maiden may symbolize the self-identification of a social group called a clan with an animal, which it may regard as its physical ancestor. As the referent of the myth is society itself, so are the symbols of religion essentially traceable to social interaction.[3] Or, ritual may be the referent of mythological symbolism, which itself may be related to social forces, psychological mechanisms, or metaphysical insight. The view that the referent of the symbol is a certain social situation must argue for an identification of similar appearing social phenomena in the same way myth elements are compared and related.

Religion is a cultural universal, and as such may be schematically classified:

> Though religion cannot be defined in terms of belief, it is none the less true that the religions of primitive people tend to cluster around a number of typical beliefs or classes of belief. It will be quite impossible to give even a superficial account of the many types of religious belief that have been reported for primitive man, and I shall therefore be content with a brief mention of three of them, belief in spirits (animism), belief in gods, and belief in cosmic power (mana).[4]

These categories have been subject to intensive argument. Each one of them has been claimed as "most basic" to all religious activity. Supernaturalism may be seen as the underlying belief common to all of them, and for our purposes will suffice to serve as the basic factor.

The aim of religion is to solve two problems: that of relating man to the universe conceptually (and emotionally) —(which becomes the philosophical pursuit of metaphysics in secularized society), and that of controlling the natural or superhuman forces in the universe—which is to say magic.[5] Sir James Frazer argued that magic becomes science when false principles of control are replaced with valid ones based on physical law; and that magic is not only separate from religion, but historically preceded religion. Although these two aspects of Frazer's theory of magic have now been rejected (the term "magico-religious" is sometimes used in modern writing to indicate the inseparability of relationship) his clarification of the principles of magic is still found useful:

> If we analyse the principles of thought on which magic is based, they will probably be found to resolve themselves into two: first, that like produced like, or that an effect resembles its cause; and, second, that things which have once been in contact with each other continue to act on each other at a distance

after the physical contact has been severed. The former principle may be called the Law of Similarity, the latter the Law of Contact or Contagion.[6]

It may be convenient to tabulate as follows the branches of magic according to the laws of thought which underlie them:[7]

Sympathetic Magic
(Law of Sympathy)

Homeopathic Magic   Contagious Magic
(Law of Similarity)   (Law of Contact)

In *The Golden Bough* Frazer lists hundreds of examples of magical practices falling into these categories, collected from all over the world. The essential error in his thinking was assuming the "intellectualism" of primitive man. Frazer conceived of his principles of magic as rising from "laws of thought" which distinguished them from the irrational practices of religion. As later writers have shown,[8] in the minds of the individuals involved there has seldom been any actual separation of magical and religious practice. The principles of magic developed from complex emotional attitudes and culturally-determined semi-empirical observations.

Magic is linked with tabu, which is prohibition of certain actions to avoid unfavorable results. Frazer's view of tabu as negative magic—that is, implicit cause-and-effect sequences based on magical principles of sympathy which are avoided, rather than manipulated, to control the universe—has been qualified to show that the religious spirit of awe is sometimes attached to the immeasurable danger behind the forbidden acts, although many tabu formulas—such as forbidding crossed legs and tied knots in a room in which childbirth is imminent—are of the "calculated risk" variety.

Tabu is, in its turn, often linked with totemism. A clan not only identifies itself with an animal in name, but in some cultures it is tabu to kill or eat the beast. A number of magical tabu responsibilities inhere on the clan member regarding his totemic crest. It is difficult to make the linkage hold, because anthropologists are by no means agreed that the typical totemic situation involves the tabu aspects—and totemism has appeared in many cultures (the Haida being one) in which no tabus or magical relationships between the clan and the totem beast are recognized. The necessity of a relation between clan society and totemism is also open to some doubt. Boas pointed out that "The recognition of kinship groups, and with it of exogamy, is a universal phenomenon. Totemism is not."[9] His view of the fundamental function of totemism was simply that it served as a label to distinguish between "incest groups." The use of animal names for these labels was somewhat arbitrary.

The concept of totemism as being a necessary aspect of exogamic clan-structure society has linked it with the matrilineal family system in the theories of cultural evolution. Evolutionary schemes for the development of the family start with the assumption that marital arrangements were unstable in archaic times. Boas writes,

> Where . . . marital conditions were unstable and the women remained members of the parental economic group, maternal descent was the only one possible. . . . When . . . property right in agricultural land prevailed, the man may have joined the woman's group and a maternal family would have developed.[10]

Evolutionists assumed that for Europe and the Near East, at least, the progress from "promiscuous" to matrilineal family systems was universal and that exogamic totemic clans were the next step toward patrilineal descent. In Europe, the reasoning goes, matrilineal descent was also linked to the female control of economic factors in early agricultural society. Thus a matriarchy would be a society controlled politically and economically by women, with a religion oriented toward female high deities. Anthropologists today deny that full matriarchy ever existed in fact, but matrilineal descent and mother-goddess worship was common if not universal at one time in Europe and the Near East. According to evolutionary theory, this totemic period was full of survivals from the earlier mother-oriented level, which are mostly commonly seen in mythological references and ritual-religious observances. Some of these even survived into the later mythology of the patrilineal Greeks, who were already unaware of the derivation of their gods and goddesses by historic times. The submergence of matrilineal society in Europe and the Near East has been attributed to the gradual increase of wealth which agricultural technology provided, combined with the invention of the plow which—by virtue of the superior strength required to wield it—took agricultural activities out of the hands of the women. Males wanted their wealth to descend to their biological children rather than to those of the maternal uncles (as it does in Haida society) and so had to break "maternal law." Friedrich Engels, whose study of anthropology was largely derived from the work of L. H. Morgan,[11] called this a "revolution—one of the most radical ever experienced by humanity."[12] It was accomplished by simply abolishing the tracing of descent by female lineage and substituting male descent. A similar theory argues that this process was aided considerably by the invasion of patrilineal Indo-Aryans who poured out of western Central Asia into the Mediterranean and the Indus valley region of India between 1400 and 1200 B.C., overwhelming these stable, matrilineal civilizations. Heinrich Zimmer writes, in his discussion of pre-Aryan Indian religion,

> And so it now appears that though the earliest literary evidence of the existence of the goddess Lotus-Shri-Lakshmi is a late and apocryphal hymn attached to the Aryan corpus of the Rig-Veda, this mother of the world was actually supreme in India long before the arrival of the conquerors from the north. The occlusion of the Indus civilization together with its goddess queen must have resulted from the arrival of the strictly patriarchal warrior-herdsmen, and the installation of their patriarchal gods.[13]

The goddess Lotus-Shri-Lakshmi, Zimmer tells us, is a

> . . . special aspect or local development of the Mother Earth of
> old: the great mother goddess of the Chalcolithic period, who
> was worshipped over a wide area of the world, and of whom
> innumerable images have been found throughout the ancient
> near East, in the lands of the Mediterranean, the Black Sea, and
> in the Danube valley. She is a sister, or double, of the well-
> known goddesses of early Sumero-Semitic Mesopotamia; and
> thus she furnished a clew to pre-Aryan linkages between India
> and the sources of our Western tradition of myth and symbol.[14]

The rituals and worship of this goddess, which will be dis-
cussed more fully later, may be seen as a highly concentra-
ted convergence of the magico-religious beliefs presented
here, and were closely connected with the beliefs and motifs found in archaic European and Mediterranean mythology.

To return to a discussion of the Swan-Maiden myth
itself: Hartland sees (with a strong evolutionary bias) the
tale as moving through stages similar to cultures—the most
primitive types being those in which human beings marry
real beasts (as in the Bear-wife story of the Kwakiutl Indians); the versions in which she changes shape and lives in
human form with her husband, a higher stage; the feather-
robe motif a purification of this; and the ultimate height
being situations of human-husband-divine-wife marriage
without any animal form intruding. Since the myth commonly centers around the Swan-Maiden incident and her
transformations, however, this is the most significant level
of the myth for comparative study, and is indicative of its
underlying relation to totemism. The Swan-Maiden myth is,
in Hartland's view, a somewhat rationalized explanation of
the clan totem. The clan is said to be descended from a
Swan (or other bird) and the conditions of the original hu-
man-animal intercourse which made this possible are described in the myth:

> . . . we have found some of the Swan-maiden tales bodly pro-

fessing to account for the worship of totems; and so thoroughly does totemism appear to be ingrained in the myth that there is some reason for thinking that here we have a clue to the myth's origin and meaning.[15]

MacCulloch finds the core of the myth in the robe or skin-stealing incidents:

. . . in these there seems to lie the key to the whole group—the idea that for one person to gain possession of an article of clothing, ornament, hair or nail clippings, or even to learn the secret name of another person, brings that person within his power. . . . With the weakening of such beliefs, the story would be told of supernatural women only, and it was now influenced by stories of the totemistic Beast Marriage group, in which a wife is both animal and human, and can take human form at will. When the incidents of this last group of tales were attracted into the group which told of a woman captured because a man gained possession of her garment or the like, the totemistic origin of the Beast Marriage stories had been long forgotten. But the animal skin now took the place of the garment. Two story-groups thus coalesced as neatly as do the animal and human natures in the Swan-maiden.[16]

These discussions are extremely vague and of little value in determining place of origin. To discover the actual conditions of the growth and meaning of the myth elements—even in a comparative sense—would require more precise historical location of the Swan-Maiden tale's place of birth. To do so accurately is almost impossible, but one may make the attempt.

Three sources of European folklore can be roughly distinguished: the Indo-Aryan tradition of tales which may be traced from India to Scandinavia; the Celtic; and the pre-Aryan Mediterranean. It has often been claimed that the majority of present-day folk literature, particularly *märchen*, comes from the Indo-Aryan tradition with borrowing from Greek and Roman mythology. Theodore Benfey was one of the most persistent adherents to this view. Today India is viewed as "a source of many stories but . . . only one of

several great centers of invention and dissemination." [17]
Since the Swan-Maiden myth shows considerable corres-
pondence with Greek and Celtic myth-forms, and the India
which Benfey derived his tales from was the Aryan India of
patrilineal family structure, I shall tentatively accept the
possibility of an assocation between matrilineal descent, the
religious and ritual practices sometimes associated with it,
and the supernatural marriage and quest tale motifs. This
would indicate the Mediterranean as the ultimate home of
the Swan-Maiden myth elements, if not the complete form.
It has been argued that the tale may be traced to Celtic
mythology. Connection between the Swan-Maiden children
in medieval romances and Celtic folklore has been made by
Hibbard:

> The ancient Celtic tale of the Children of Lir, now known only
> in eighteenth-century texts, attributes the transformation of the
> children to the hostile magic of a stepmother who is jealous of
> their father's love for them. [18]

Hartland connects a later Welsh tale, "The Lady of the Van
Pool," involving marriage between a man and a supernatural woman who appears in a pool, with both the Swan-Maid-
en story and the Lady of the Lake of Arthurian romance
fame. [19] Both connections seem entirely possible, and if at
all valid, they open an immense series of correlations which
leads—eventually—to the Mediterranean. Roger Loomis has
demonstrated very convincingly, in an argument to which I
cannot possibly do justice, the Celtic derivation of Arthurian romance, particularly as it centers around the Grail
Quest. He then derives pre-Christian Celtic mythology from
pre-Aryan Mediterranean ritual: [20]

> By a strange coincidence, not only the mythical elements of
> the Grail legend, but also the ritual elements confused with
> them are accounted for by the cults of Samothrace, for they
> seem to supply the prototype of the Grail Bearer. The Great
> Earth-Mother was worshipped at Samothrace, not only as De-
> meter and Hecate, but also as Cybele, whose original cult center

was in Asia Minor. It is known that in her mysteries a priestess bore on her head a krater (the very word from which the word Grail is ultimately derived), usually called the *kernos*, to each side of which a lamp was attached—a reminder of the candles which nearly always attended to the Grail Bearer. The contents of the *kernos* are supposed by the best scholars to have been of a distinctly sexual nature.[21]

. . . If we combine the myths about Demeter and Iasion with the mysteries of Cybele and Attis, we can explain an incredible number of features in the Grail legends. . . .

The report preserved by Strabo that in an island near Britain sacrifices were offered to Demeter and Kore like those of Samothrace finds an incredible amount of corroboration in Arthurian romance. For the corresponding divinity, who must have sprung from ancient mythological roots which ran deep in the soil of the British Isles, and whom we can trace back to Wales and Ireland, shares six characteristics with the Greek goddesses. She is the heroine of a seasonal abduction story. She is mistress both of moon and vegetation. She transforms herself from the most hideous animal-like forms to radiant beauty. She is a guide to the Other World. She embraces a youthful god with the knowledge of her husband, who interrupts them with his lightning stroke.[22]

Gawain, whom Loomis sees as the key actor in the cycle, is derived from the ancient Celtic sun-god Curoi. The many loves of Gawain are essentially the same entity:

. . . they are but different manifestations, different names for the same primeval divinity, whose power is felt in the mysterious influences of the moon, and whose beauty in the golden gorse and yellow fields of wheat. She has always borne many names: Isis, Europa, Artemis, Rhea, Demeter, Hecate, Persephone, Diana, . . .[23]

Celtic mythology and the myths of Greece, it is then possible, both rose from prototypes shaped by the worship of the Great Mother. Her religion and ritual produced a series of legends in which she assumed many animal and human forms and married human men who were killed or died.

Such are the stories of Cybele and Attis, Venus and Adonis, Demeter and Iasion, and Blodeuedd and Gronw. From these recurrent myth forms—which have been compiled in both ritual and literary versions by Frazer—the Swan Maiden's marriage with a human spouse took form and went into oral literature, to travel all over the globe. The swan or bird form may not be entirely accidental in the background of the myth, for the goddess often took bird form—there were bird-cults associated with her worship[24] and some specific symbolism may be tentatively produced:

> The Three Nymphs must be understood as the Three Graces, that is to say, the Triple-Love-goddess. The Gracae were also known as the Phorcides, which means the daughters of Phorcus, or Orcus, and according to Scholiast on Aeschylus had the form of swans—which is probably an error for cranes, due to a mis-reading of a sacred picture, since cranes and swans, *equally sacred birds*, are alike flying in V-formation. They were, in fact, the Three Fates.[25]

Implicit in many of the arguments produced here is the belief that mythology has a special relation to ritual,[26] and is usually derived from it. Boas and others have adequately shown that in North America, at least, they have a tendency to reinforce, describe, and occasionally alter each other, with no possibility of determining which is basic to the other. Frazer's examples of ritual-and-myth interplay in the Mediterranean, in *The Golden Bough*, may indicate for that region chronological precedence of ritual over certain myths dealing with supernatural marriage, death of the divine lover (the dying god) and his (or her, as in the myth of the Kore) resurrection from the underworld and reappearance in reborn form on earth. The death and rebirth of the god/goddess, as is well known, was correlated with the seasonal death and return of the crops by Frazer. The death and rebirth aspect of the supernatural-marriage motif may perhaps be seen as the form behind the loss and regaining motif of the Swan-Maiden tale. The Mediterranean versions of the myth refer not to nature itself, but to nature through the medium of the ritual drama. The ritual was a community-acted magical operation guaranteeing fertility (control of the universe). In this three-way relationship of myth-ritual-nature, in terms of human activity, the ritual was the hub.

3. DIFFICULTIES OF THE COMPARATIVE METHOD

As has been noted before, the assumption in the method I have been relying on is that cultures develop in a parallel fashion through similar evolutionary stages, and that for this reason similar customs and myth incidents may be validly compared as to psychic content as well as outward form. This is anything but true. I shall briefly cite the major criticisms of the comparative method as they relate to mythology:

> Historical inquiry shows that similar ideas do not always arise from the same preceding conditions . . . either their suggested identity does not exist or the similarity of form is due to an assimilation of phenomena that are distinct in origin, but develop under similar social stress.[27]

Boas fully documents his stand with examples from American Indian material. "Ethnic phenomena which we compare are seldom really alike,"[28] he writes, and clarifies his view of psychic unity:

> I do believe in the existence of analogous psychical processes among all races wherever analogous social conditions prevail; but I do not believe that ethnic phenomena are simply expressions of these psychological laws.

> . . . the selection of material assembled for the purpose of comparison is wholly determined by the subjective point of view according to which we arrange diverse mental phenomena. In order to justify our inference that these phenomena are the same, the comparability has to be proved by other means. This has never been done.[29]

This means that although the outward form of a myth may seem similar to those found in other cultures, the meaning projected into the symbolic framework provided by the type form varies, in more than just matters of place names, animal species, and references to cultural usages. As an example, the "Girl and the Dog" myth of North America may be cited. It is a story in which a dog assumes human form and marries a girl. According to T. T. Waterman it

> is told on the plains of North America merely as an interesting tale. Among the Eskimo it is told in connection with a story explaining the existence of sea-mammals, and the most important single factor in the life of the people; it supplies the background for the chief feature of their religion, the seal taboos. On the North Pacific coast also it has a religious application, accounting for or explaining a certain religious taboo and the origin of a secret society.[30]

Thompson has similar criticism, particularly of the comparative study of motifs—which has been my main approach in this chapter:

> This interest in motifs, rather than in complete tales, is, in fact, characteristic of all those scholars who seek to find some general principle by which to explain the origin of tale-telling as a human activity.[31]

He goes on to point out that comparative study of motifs can be bent to prove virtually anything, if one fails to take into account the principle of convergence: that motifs and myths take similar form for different reasons, and that disparate psychological content is then attached to them. The fact of convergence does not destroy the possibility of investigation of ultimate causes, but turns the focus of attention away from social forms and customs to the psychological process of myth formation itself. Boas believe that "imagination" is the basic mental activity to mythology, but as psychologists—and since I. A. Richards, literary critics— know, imagination is a very complex and somewhat variable activity. The psychoanalysts, with a rather special theory of imagination, have also undertaken myth study. Their basis of approach is—as Thompson drily noted—dreams. The most common error of psychological myth study is taking "a given myth pretty much for granted as a reasonably self-consistent psychic formation."[32] Historical study shows the random, chance grouping of elements that may destroy the psychologist's psychic structure. Nonetheless, as Boas ruefully admits, the psychologist has a place in mythological studies, and at present he will probably prove to be a psychoanalyst.

Edward Sapir described two types of psychological myth study: one deals with "the psychic significance, conscious or unconscious, of the single elements of mythology" —the motifs. The other he calls:

> . . . the cumulative psychology of myth as a particlar social pattern. . . . It is the psychology that will some day underlie the study of all culture-history for it manifests itself across generations in a persistent striving of form . . . the first requisite of a psychological understanding of mythology—of other phases of culture as well—is the discovery of a social psychology of "form-libido."[33]

Our historical study is not rendered completely useless, then, for although we know that the content attached to Swan-Maiden mythology from the worship of many-breasted Cybele to the Haida Indians has varied tremendously, the forms themselves have recurred—a fact which in itself is significant. Freudian theorists, whose work will be cited next, believe that an unconscious level of content attaches to these myths wherever they occur which cannot be explicated in terms of the culture and the apparent culture-meaning of the myth, but may be seen in the relation of myth-images to dreams.

4. THE MYTH AS ARCHETYPICAL IMAGES

It is impossible to outline the history of psychoanalytic

theory here. It may be briefly stated that Freudians postulate the intensely formative nature of childhood experience as it revolves around the child-parent relationship, and the potential blocks to satisfaction of that relationship as almost inherent in the family situation. This gives rise to the Oedipus complex. The action of these experiences on the adult individual, however, takes place through the "unconscious" part of the mind so that the individual is seldom aware of the motivating experiences behind his acts, and tends to associate other causes with them in his conscious mind. In social life, the individual acts toward the group in terms of his relationship to his mother in childhood. The unconscious most often makes itself known in dreams—which are visual images. Even more elaborate fantasies of conscious construction—such as myths—draw on the unconscious images. Basic experiences are projected, thus, as images or symbolic situations into mythology.[34]

C.G. Jung, whose work has most application here, plays down Freud's emphasis on the sexual nature of the basic experiences and extends the realm of the unconscious to contain a vast storehouse of images based not only on the individual's formative experience, but on the basic experience of all humanity. He sees this psychological content as inherited, and terms it the *collective unconscious*. Sapir sums up the Jungian concept of how this collective unconscious manifests itself in contemporary culture:

> The resemblance between the content of primitive rituals—and symbolic behavior generally among primitive peoples—and the apparently private rituals and symbolisms developed by those who have greater than normal difficulty in adjusting to their social environment are said to be so numerous and far-reaching that the latter must be looked upon as an inherited survival of more archaic types of thought and feeling.[35]

Jung's term for the images that recur both in the psyche and in myths is archetype:

> . . . mythological components which, because of their typical

nature, we can call "motif," primordial images, types or—as I have named them—archetypes. . . . Today we can hazard the formula that the archetypes appear in myths and fairy-tales just as they do in dreams and in the products of psychotic fantasy.[36]

Jung's interpretation of the goddess-mother on these principles is contained in an essay entitled "The Psychological Aspects of the Kore."[37] Although he bases his study on the Demeter-Kore myth, he is aware that historically the three goddesses described in the Greek version—Demeter goddess of fertility, Persephone or Kore, the maiden, and Hecate, goddess of death and the underworld—were fragmented from the earlier single goddess who was maid, mother, and hag in one,[38] and sees this triple identification as being central to the psychological meaning. The Kore "in its threefold aspect of maiden, mother, and Hecate is not unknown to the psychology of the unconscious"[39] and is a product of feminine experience-projection, rather than masculine. "The man's role in the Demeter myth is really only that of seducer or conqueror."[40] Even in contemporary images the Kore appears occasionally in animal form. Jung cites dreams of his patients to show the similarity between the dream images and the forms assumed historically by the goddess. For the man, the Demeter-Kore figure appears as the projection of his own mother—beneficent and forbidding at once, but for the woman

Demeter-Kore exists on the plane of mother-daughter experience, which is alien to man and shuts him out. In fact, the psychology of the Demeter cult has all the features of a matriarchal order of society where the man is indispensable but on the whole a disturbing factor.[41]

This brief presentation of Jung's theory of the mother goddess indicates a potential reason for the popularity of the Swan Maiden herself—particularly as she appears in those versions in which she enigmatically gives in to the man, only to leave him for a slight reason and require an elaborate and dangerous journey of him before returning. The ambiguous nature of the Swan Maiden, and her ultimate unapproach-ableness, gives her psychological as well as historical relationship to the goddess prototype. The maiden is too small a unit, however, to be of any real value in studying the total Swan-Maiden structure, particularly if it is to be eventually related to the Haida version. For this reason, we shall move to a Jungian-based study of the total form—the quest myth —in which the maiden is only one motif.

5. THE MYTH AS ARCHETYPAL FORM

Joseph Campbell sees in the quest myth pattern a symbolic significance which corresponds on the one hand to primitive rites of initiation, and on the other to the psychological journey into the unconscious required of the individual who would attain "wholeness" in the complete sense of the reconciliation of opposites. In all effective mythology, the quest motif is the key:

> The standard path of the mythological adventure of the hero is a magnification of the formula represented in the rites of passage: *separation—initiation—return*: which might be named the nuclear unit of the monomyth. A hero ventures forth from the world of common day into a region of supernatural wonder: fabulous forces are there encountered and a decisive victory is won: the hero comes back from this mysterious adventure with the power to bestow boons on his fellow man.[42]

Within this framework fits the supernatural marriage, otherworld journey, and regaining of lost wife. In the psychological journey, the tests are self-imposed blocks to the world-transcending enlightenment which is almost the Zen Buddhist type of enlightenment—a sense of complete identification with the universe.[43] The boon may be—as in the Demeter-Kore myth, the return of fertility to the soil; or in the psychological manifestation, creative fruition. Campbell is very explicit about the relation between the journey of the hero, and that of the soul:

It is the business of mythology proper, and of the fairy tale, to reveal the specific dangers and techniques of the dark interior way from tragedy to comedy. Hence the incidents are fantastic and "unreal": they represent psychological, not physical triumphs. Even when the legend is of an actual historical personage, the deeds of victory are rendered, not in lifelike, but in dreamlike configurations. . . .

The passage of the mythological hero may be overground, incidentally: fundamentally it is inward—into depths where obscure resistances are overcome, and long lost, forgotten powers are revivified, to be made available for the transfiguration of the world.[44]

Woman, in the quest myth, symbolizes "the totality of what can be known" and the sacred marriage of the myth, particularly as represented in the Mediterranean versions, is the identification of self and father-image. "The mystical marriage with the Queen Goddess of the world represents the hero's total mastery of life . . . he and the father are one. He is in the father's place."[45] Thus is the Oedipus complex overcome.

The Haida version clearly fits within the pattern. Even the hero's end as seagull may be explained: having reached the ultimate boon of knowledge in regaining his wife, there is no more need to communicate with his own people, and he has—in psychological sense—been reborn and taken new form. As seagull, he has symbolically transcended his old ordinary human self.

The intrinsic value of the symbolic form is seen to be its metaphorical approximation of a common psychological process of personality integration. The images within it are based on projections of the collective or individual unconscious. In Jungian terms, then, the popularity of the Swan-Maiden myth is based on the way it dovetails with basic mental processes, and although to the cultures who tell and transmit its versions this is not apparent, it fulfills psychological needs which makes them turn to its form and images again and again.

The latent psychic content is difficult to locate in terms of any one specific myth. This theory is thus seldom useful in the practical study of distribution, which is concerned with processes of repetition, adoption, incorporation, combination on account of similarities, transfusion of elements, metathesis (in which the hero of one version becomes the ogre of another) and alteration of explanatory content.[46] Sapir's critique in incisive:

> Symbols, like other accepted forms, are ready to receive whatever psychic content the individual psychology or social psychology of a given time and place is prepared to put into them. Myths may or may not have been motivated by certain unconscious trends, but it is difficult to understand how they could indefinitely keep their significance as symbols of these trends.[47]

The popularity of the Swan-Maiden myth has been seen as the product of universal social institutions, psychological images, and latent identification with the processes of the form. There is little more to be said about underlying causes at the present stage of myth scholarship; the problem of the recurrent, flexible form of quest myths and their multiple levels of significance is still vital, if unsolved.

I offer the following table as a schematic outline of the symbolic equivalences that may be seen in the myth-type as they coincide in the seasons, rituals, and individual psychological processes, to sum up the levels of significance modern scholars have seen. These correspondences are purely metaphorical, and are based on Frazer's correlation of the seasons with rituals, the rituals with aspects of the quest-myth form; and Campbell's correlation of the quest-myth form with psychological activity, and the further connection that may be seen with theological psychology (Death-in-life and Life-in-death).

Type: Hero's birth, marriage to supernatural wife, loss of wife, quest for wife, eventual recovery, and death of the hero.

1. Hero's birth: found on waves, son of peasant, etc.	Individual body comes from womb; Differentiation of group from mankind. Earth takes form from primal ocean. Crops from soil. VERNAL EQUINOX
2. Marriage to supernatural wife.	Individual identifies self with group. Sense of brotherhood. Ritual insight. Marriage of sun and earth. Maturity of crops. SUMMER SOLSTICE
3. Loss of wife: through insulting, breaking a tabu, etc.	Conflict with group. Id vs. superego. Loss of self-identity with group, and consequent dissociation of personality. "Death in Life." Death of vegetation. AUTUMN EQUINOX
4. Quest for wife: involving journey and dangerous tests.	Recognition of psychological loss and willed attempt to recover basic insight —epiphanic (solitary) insight as contrasted to ritual (group) insight. Tests as internal blocks. Group seeks reorientation. Winter hardship eliminates biologically unfit; earth dormant, sun at its farthest reach. "Purgatory."
5. Recovery of wife and death or transformation of hero.	Enlightenment. Personality integration. Merging of ritual and epiphanic insights. Death of illusory motives destroys possibility of participating in world of illusion, hence transformation and "Life in Death." Also rebirth in form of son, which may be seen as the individual will to return and act

in the world of people asserting itself.
Cf. Frazer's Priest of Nemi, "He who
slays and will be slain." New life ger-
mane in seed below ground. Earth
quickens and the old has died off, to
be replaced by the new.
WINTER SOLSTICE

Although occasional contradictions may be found in
this table, it serves to outline the most obvious equivalences.

The study of the Swan-Maiden myth as literature—in
its symbolic form and in the Haida version itself, may make
it possible to see how the symbolism acts on levels of imagery and language, and afford new insight into the nature
of the form, and eventually the final problem—that of the
myth's actual function in society. The relationships between
the cultural and comparative aspects of the Haida versions
and the problems outlined in this chapter to literary criticism will be shown in the next chapter, with—as will be
seen—the highest blessings of several scholars.

CHAPTER V

THE MYTH AS LITERATURE

1. INTRODUCTORY

Even if the potential historical sources of the Haida Swan-
Maiden myth cited in the last chapter were demonstrably
valid, they would contribute little to the understanding of
the Haida version itself. As the archaic embodiments of symbolic themes of psychological importance, which the Haida
version also contains, they would be of interest—but the
main point of attack in a study designed to understand the
Swan-Maiden myth would have to be the themes, not the
proto-versions. There is too much of a gap between cultures
of the ancient Near East and that of the Haida to make generalizations about individual versions for both areas. Whatever historical connection may exist is too remote to be of
concern. One is forced to speak, not of what is held in common between the cultures[1] but what is held in common in
the myths—and that in its simplest, archetypal forms.

Regardless of the questionable validity of Jung's theories of archetypal significance, the existence of the archetype cannot be denied. The archetype is to be distinguished from Aarne's type as being a more generalized image or pattern of narrative relationships common to many types, with no assumption of historical relationship. It exists on the level of formal similiarity. The fact that myths and tales never physically exist but in individually told, stylistically complete versions, does not destroy the validity of a classificatory mode of existence for these similarities. Jung has defended the term on these grounds:

> Critics have contented themselves with asserting that no such archetypes exist. Certainly they do not exist, any more than a botanical system exists in nature! But will any one deny the existence of natural plant-families on that account? Or will any one deny the occurrence and continual repetition of certain morphological and functional similarities?[2]

Any theory which would assert the importance of comparative myth study in the understanding of actual versions must demonstrate not only what appears to be universally meaningful in the archetype, but must somehow show the action of archetypal imagery on the many aspects of the version's narrative form. This study of the interplay between archetypes and individual versions, concerned as it must be with stylistic-formal aspects, is necessarily a literary study—drawing on concepts developed in Western literary scholarship to make its material intelligible. Such study must start with the individual version and investigate the historical connections, formal similarities, and underlying archetype of the myth—which I have already done with the Haida myth —and try to relate this to what is known of the myth's many culturally determined aspects, which include the attitudes toward mythology and the standards of literary evaluation, that demand that oral literature contain certain technical devices. Such completeness of scholarship has never been practiced on oral literature. Franz Boas, in *Tsimshian Mythology*, did the most complete single study to date, but his investigation was primarily concerned with the cultural side of the Tsimshian folk literature—specifically material culture and social organization. His comparative study is extraordinarily thorough, but limited to the Northwest Coast and related areas. Stylistic and linguistic considerations are excluded. As it is, the book runs to 1037 quarto pages, of which only 334 are actual myth-texts.

In this chapter I will describe the literary significance of archetypes related to the Haida myth, then discuss distinctive aspects of oral literature, and the Haida myth as literature in translation, and conclude with the problem of the relation of archetype and version.

2. THE ARCHETYPES AND LITERATURE

The archetypes discovered in the historical sources described in the last chapter have been extensively related, by some scholars, to the Western literary tradition. According to Robert Graves, the literary significance of this material is responsible for the most effective poetry in that tradition:

> My thesis is that the language of poetic myth anciently current in the Mediterranean and Northern Europe was a magical language bound up with popular religious ceremonies in honour of the Moon-goddess, or Muse, some of them dating from the Old Stone Age, and that this remains the language of true poetry—"true" in the nostalgic modern sense of "the unimprovable original, not a synthetic substitute." The language was tampered with in late Minoan times when invaders from Central Asia began to substitute patrilineal for matrilineal institutions and remodel or falsify the myths to justify the social changes.
> . . . the ancient language survived purely enough in the secret Mystery-cults of Eleusis, Corinth, Samothrace and elsewhere; and when these were suppressed by the early Christian Emperors it was still taught in the poetic colleges of Ireland and Wales, and in the witch-covens of Western Europe. As a popular religious tra-

dition it finally flickered out at the close of the seventeenth century. . . .[3]

This tradition contains, for Graves, the "one poetic Theme"—

> . . . the antique story, which falls into thirteen chapters and an epilogue, of the birth, life, death and resurrection of the God of the Waxing Year; the central chapters concern the God's losing battle with the God of the Waning Year for love of the capricious and all-powerful Threefold Goddess, their mother, bride and layer-out. The poet identifies himself with the God of the Waxing Year and his Muse with the Goddess; the rival is his blood-brother, his other self, his weird. All true poetry—true by Housman's practical test—celebrates some incident or scene in this very ancient story, and the three main characters are so much a part of our racial inheritance that they not only assert themselves in poetry, but recur in occasions of emotional stress in the form of dreams, paranoiac visions, and delusions.[4]

In Graves' identification with the psychological action of the Goddess with a "racial inheritance" and dreams, we see the theory of the collective unconscious tacitly admitted. In the Haida version, if one draws out the obvious similarities, the hero parallels the God of the Waxing Year, the Swan Maiden the Threefold Goddess.

Joseph Campbell's analysis of the quest-myth in many ways parallels Graves' thesis. Although Campbell makes no attempt at tracing historical relationships as Graves does, his reliance on Jung is similar, and his insistence on the importance of the quest-myth and the images it encompasses as basic to literature almost parallels Graves:

> Whether we listen with aloof amusement to the dreamlike mumbo jumbo of some red-eyed witch doctor of the Congo, or read with cultivated rapture thin translations from the sonnets of the mystic Lao-tse, or now and again crack the hard nutshell of an argument of Aquinas, or catch suddenly the shining meaning of a bizarre Eskimo fairy tale, it will always be one, shape-shifting yet marvelously constant story that we find, together with a challengly persistent suggestion of more remaining to be experienced than will ever be known or told.[5]

The actual effectiveness of this "constant story" depends more on its literary context than Campbell seems willing to admit, although Graves considers the theme rather fragile, and admits that a trained poetic technique is required in properly presenting it. It is clear that the archetype as such need not be good literature. The plot "Boy meets Girl, Boy loses Girl, Boy wins Girl back," is a stock formula for modern magazine stories; and it could be shown to be merely another manifestation of the quest-myth archetype. It would take considerable ingenuity to prove each such story or novel a work of great art. In the skill of the artistic presentation, the archetype is empowered to communicate whatever hidden significance it may possess to the unsuspecting reader or hearer. To understand the nature of such skill in the Haida version requires some knowledge of oral literature.

3. THE MYTH AS ORAL LITERATURE

Since oral literature is carried in memory alone, it is impossible to expect any single version—whether myth, tale, fable, riddle, proverb, or song, to stay the same indefinitely. Even so, the tenacity of oral material is sometimes amazing. The process of transmission has many versions of comparatively few types—or if Campbell's view is accepted, of one archetype. The operation of memory in oral literature is something of a cultural variable—in societies valuing word-perfect renderings of myths or tales—such as the ancient Welsh, Irish, and Icelandic have been described to be—individual tellers mastered hundreds of tales without deviating from the accepted story in any detail. Even in less specialized cultures, tales may sometimes show little change through time. Boas describes a minor tale known by both Labrador and Cumberland Sound Eskimo, widely separated peoples:

> . . . Even the names of the heroes are the same in these tales. Since intercourse between the regions where these tales were

collected is very slight,—in fact, ceased several centuries ago, —we must conclude that even these trifling stories are old. In fact, their great similarity arouses the suspicion that many of the apparently trifling tales of war and hunting, of feats of shamans and of starvation, may be quite old.[6]

A culture may have a very rich literary tradition entirely in orally transmitted material. Bascom estimates a minimum of five thousand tales for the Yoruba of Africa in oral tradition.[7]

Processes of change and transmission are very complex. In the simplest sense details of change may be seen as due either to some determining factor within the tale, or to some determining factor in the culture. The stylistic demands of oral literature were noted by Paul Radin in 1915, when he wrote an essay outlining these influences and criticizing the orientation of folklore scholars at that time:

> All these studies have . . . for the most part concerned themselves with a mechanical analysis of myths and the tabulation of motifs, episodes, and themes of which they consisted. Most of these investigators seem, however, to have been quite oblivious of the implications necessarily entailed by the recognition that in primitive mythology we are dealing often with literature in the true sense of the word.[8]

> To me the reasons for the differences in the various versions of the same myth or tale are due mainly to certain literary tendencies at work.[9]

> . . . a certain amount of variability found in versions of the same myth or tale is due to the influence of different types of plot elaboration, which in turn is due to the artistic individuality of the raconteur.[10]

Radin demonstrates how the same plot (or type) may be handled by three different modes of narrative: the sequence of events being "brought about by the actions of the actors themselves without the intermediation of a figure foretelling the various episodes" as in the Haida version of the Swan-

80

Maiden myth—and most other versions cited here—or the plot is "outlined beforehand by some individuals and the episodes appear in full force only then; or, finally, the plot is developed in the form of a dialogue."[11] The same myth, presented in each of these ways, shows differences which make each presentation a separate version—entirely because of the mode of telling. Radin's analysis is by no means complete, but it suggests the possibility of a very complex and seldom obvious tendency of the formal aspects in oral literature to determine the nature of redactions.

The cultural factors which determine stylistic aspects of oral literature include the preexisting body of oral literature when any new tale is introduced. Similar elements may be incorporated, and adopted tales so completely combined as to give no evidence to the anthropologist of its origin. Explanatory (etiological) tags, as Waterman has show, are usually appended to tales already in circulation, and are not essential to myth formation. "The story is the original thing, the explanation an afterthought."[12] Much the same process is responsible for the ritualization of myths—a process whereby tales originally borrowed from an alien group become part of the religious outlook through recasting, and are dramatized in ritual or held to account for a ritual which was preexistent in the borrowing culture. In this way, the Swan-Maiden story is a myth or tale depending entirely on the integration of the version into the projective life of its tellers. An example of this process within our own culture can be seen in contemporary attitudes toward the Bible: the story of Adam and Eve is often held to be an entertaining fiction, but at one time it was the accepted account of the beginning of all humanity and was believed to be a literal statement from God. The narrative itself has not changed in this shifting of values. The Adam and Eve incident has even been incorporated (from missionary influence) by several primitive cultures into preexisting mythologies and become part of an entirely different cosmogony. The narrative itself contains the germs of new significance when it becomes translated and told in a new society, stripped of all its old associations.

Stylistic complexity in oral literature is best seen in primitive song, which is usually considered the prototype of modern poetry.[13] The myths and tales considered here are closer to prose, and subject to less formal complexity. They may be nearer poetic form than written prose usually is (excluding recent writers such as Stein and Joyce) because of their dependence on rhythm. According to Boas,

> The investigation of primitive narrative as well as of poetry proves that repetition, particularly rhythmic repetition, is a fundamental trait. All prose narratives consist in part of free elements the form of which is dependent upon the taste and ability of the narrator. Inserted among these passages we find others of fixed form which give the narrative to a great extent its formal attractiveness. Quite often these passages consist of conversations between the actors in which deviation from the fixed formula is not permitted. In other cases they are of rhythmic form and must be considered poetry or chants rather than prose.[14]

Edward Sapir studied the song inserted within prose narrative, and found it to be occasionally an integral part of oral prose style:

> This is the short song inserted here and there within the body of a myth; generally intended to express some emotion or striking thought of a character. It is generally of very limited melodic range and very definite rhythmic structure. Sometimes it is quite different in character from the regular types of song in vogue, not infrequently being considered specifically appropriate to the character involved; while at other times it approximates in form such well-recognized types as the round-dance song or medicine song, according to the exigencies of the narrative. The text to such a song is very often obscure.[15]

Another type of myth narrative which is seldom studied and has no relation to our Swan-Maiden myth, is interesting for its linkage with the dream theories of Jung and Freud:

There is evidence of the existence of a second type of myth-song in America,—the song which itself narrates a myth. The most elaborate examples known of such myth-songs are the Homeric poems, which, as is well known, were sung by rhapsodists to the accompaniment of a stringed instrument. Dr. Kroeber refers to dream myths of the Mohave, that are sung by the person who has dreamt the myth.[16]

Sapir objects to limiting myth-study to the "incident or complex of incidents" and argues that, although it can seldom be seen in English translation, ". . . there is a very considerable tendency in American mythology to make characters interesting as such."[17] This is often conveyed by speech mannerisms which English cannot approximate.

Rhythm in oral narrative is seen in the frequent repetition of single motives.

> . . . the tales of the Chinook Indians are always so constructed that five brothers, one after another, have the same adventure. The four eldest perish while the youngest one comes out successful. The tale is repeated verbatim for all the brothers, and its length, which to our ears and taste is intolerable, probably gives pleasure by the repeated form.
>
> Repetitions leading to a climax are also found. Thus in Tsimshian tales an eagle is said to screech every morning. Their hero comes out of the house following the call and finds every day a larger animal on the beach in front of his house.[18]

The interaction of cultural themes, accepted formal patterns, and the symbolic framework of the myth, takes place in the creative mind of the individual narrator. The importance of the individual in oral literature is often overlooked because of his complete anonymity, yet because of the spoken nature of mythology he not only shapes the content but the form:

> The form of modern prose is largely determined by the fact that it is read, not spoken, while primitive prose is based on the art of oral delivery and is, therefore, more closely related to modern oratory than to printed literary style.[19]

The example of "modern oratory" is probably a poor one—as the dramatic possibilities of a tale give the raconteur more possibilities than the stylized rhetoric associated with old-style politicians. The raconteur is the artist—he recreates for his audience the tale as a new and unique entity each time. He is at once narrator, mime, and actor—handling all the dialogues himself. He must be aware of his necessity to act within a formal tradition:

> Every oral literature is told within the framework of an elaborate set of rules, of most of which both the raconteur and the mature members of his audience are conscious. These rules of literary form are a kind of grammar of literature, much of which is clearly recognized as such in contrast with language patterns that are for the most part not so identified.[20]

The setting in which tales and myths are recounted is also stylized:

> . . . very much as our theatre . . . with an audience and a stage. The raconteur sits or stands and recounts the myth, in a dramatic style as well as with features of verbal or literary style. The audience may have to lie or sit in a stylized position. It may have to repeat the raconteur's sentences following him, or respond in other ways.[21]

Each raconteur of skill is recognized in the group, and each one may have a distinctive style of rendition which stamps any story with his unique method.

> After many renditions his command of the tale approaches a degree of technical mastery which permits him greater freedom from mechanical matters such as memorization. He has an increasing inner assurance that he will be able to give expression to every needed word, motif, gesture, facial expression, and tone of voice. He will not err on the sequence of episodes or in building up towards the climax. The person who has achieved such technical mastery is free to "play with technique" . . . the technical master is now free to become a virtuoso or artist for the occasion.[22]

Such individuals are rare in any society, primitive or otherwise, and if given free enough play—or a specialized role, may do more with oral literature than just alter a version, or put a new twist on a motif. Each narrator may have his specific traits, as Radin has shown in his listing of the stylistic tendencies among Ojibwa raconteurs—

> . . . one man was famous for the humorous touches which he imparted to every tale; another for the fluency with which he spoke and the choice of his language; a third, for his dramatic delivery; a fourth for the radical way in which he handled time-worn themes; a fifth, for his tremendous memory; a sixth, for the accuracy with which he adhered to the "accepted" version; etc. [23]

but they shared in basic psychological qualities. The recognition of this led Radin to postulate that "among primitive peoples there exists the same distribution of ability and temperaments as among us."[24] He divides these temperaments into two types: "thinkers"—intellectuals, priests, and poets; and "actors"—warriors, chiefs, and everybody else. The thinker type, to which the raconteur belongs, is also the religious formulator, whose role is to

> . . . interpret and manipulate the psychological correlates of the economic-social realities. Stated more concretely, his task was to define and elaborate both his own viewpoint and that of the matter-of-fact man.[25]

In a culture which enables this type to flourish, he may achieve considerable power—and as priest, create elaborate systematic mythologies like one of the Polynesian cultures, or those we have evidence of once existing in the ancient Near East. "The priest or chief as poet or thinker takes hold of the folk traditions and of isolated rituals and elaborates them in dramatic and poetic form."[26]

The Haida myth, as told aloud, may have partaken of all these characteristics of oral literary performance. To what extent and how, it is impossible for us to know. Even the best phonetic rendering of a Haida language text could not convey the nuances of a raconteur's telling: a phonograph recording could not capture gestures and facial expressions. Even if these methods did hold the possibility of capturing all the charm and skill in a well-told tale, it is highly unlikely that a raconteur could do a good job before a battery of anthropologists and machines, instead of his accustomed and sympathetic audience. The excellence and beauty of folktales as oral literature is an elusive thing, something which only a few field anthropologists have witnessed. For this reason I will make no attempt at evaluating the Haida version. Conceivably someone acquainted enough with the culture and language could describe the excellence this myth achieves in the hands of a skilled narrator.[27]

The language alone poses difficult problems: linguistic studies indicate a range of possibilities in fulfilling the needs of communication quite beyond usual European conceptions. If sound is, as Bosanquet says, the "medium of poetry" and "To make poetry in different languages, e.g., in French and German, is as different a task as to make decorative work in clay and iron"[28] —then it is even more necessary to fully understand Haida (Skidegate dialect). The language in itself is a determining force on the myth. As noted, Haida belongs, in Sapir's classification, to the Nadene linguistic stock—to which Tlingit and Athabaskan also belong. Sapir's description of the stock suggests the formidable problem Haida may pose for literary scholarship:

> The *Nadene* languages, probably the most specialized of all, are tone languages and, while presenting a superficially "polysynthetic" aspect, are built up, fundamentally, of monosyllabic elements of prevailingly nominal significance which have fixed order with reference to each other and combine into morphologically loose "words"; emphasize voice and "aspect" rather than tense; make a fundamental distinction between active and static verb forms; make abundant use of post-positions after both nouns and verb forms; and compound nominal stems freely.

The radical element of these languages is probably always nominal in force and the verb is typically a derivative of a nominal base, which need not be found as such.[29]

Phonetically, Haida and other Northwest Coast languages have a number of glottalized stops and affricatives which make them difficult to pronounce for the outsider, and give the language—to Western ears—a guttural and "unpleasant" sound. Although it is not possible to show how phonetic characteristics operate on the Haida Swan-Maiden myth, to give an example of the Haida language in print I will cite a portion of another text. The alphabet used in the text is an especially designed phonetic one, which cannot be fully reproduced in a standard type font. The letters t!, s!, ts!, l!, k!, q!, are similar to t, s, ts, tc, l, k, q, but are accompanied by a catch in the breath which sometimes gives the impression of a pause, and sometimes sounds like a sharp click.[30] Apostrophes indicate a syllabic stress. A period after a letter indicates a laryngeal catch. Vowel sounds reproduced here are not equivalent to phonetic rendering, but represent the closest approximation possible, as in Italian.

Here are the first three lines of a Haida myth, text with interlinear translation, entitled Moldy-Forehead"— *Qol-q!a'lg.oda-i.*[31]

| *Nan* | *g.axa'hao* | *q! oda's* | | *gien* |
| A certain | child this | there was a famine | | when |

| *awu'n* | *at* | *q!osigwanag.an.* | | *Gie'nhao* |
| his mother | of | asked for something to eat. | | And then |

| *sqa'gi* | | *qul* | *l'* | *a'og.a* | *la* | *gi* |
| dog salmon | | upper part of | his | mother | him | for |

| *q!eitlai'yag.an* | *gien* | *g.a* | *la* | | *lt!e'ganasi.* |
| had cut off | and | in | he | | thought it was not enough. |

| *K!aa'ng.adan* | *la* | *si'usi* | *gien* | *l'* | *sg.a'-lx.idas.* |
| It was too small | he | said | and | he | began to cry. |

This may indicate something of the phonetic qualities that Haida possesses, as well as grammatical characteristics. As Boas pointed out, it is entirely possible for metaphorical expressions in an alien language to hold an intelligible content for the outsider. In Kwakiutl,

> Love is called "sickness, pain" *(ts!ex'ela)*. The lover wishes to be the bed *(ts!ag'il)* or pillow *(qe'nol)* of the beloved. To be downcast is called "to be withered" *(xwe'lsa);* to ridicule "to nettle" *(dze'nka)*.[32]

Any further discussion of the myth will have to be of the version in English translation, in terms of its availability as such to the non-Haida reader.

4. THE MYTH AS LITERATURE IN TRANSLATION

No matter how difficult it is to translate oral literature, one cannot feel that this text fulfills the possibilities of lucid expression in English. As social document, it describes the culture, and as a literal translation of what must have been a trifle vague in an elderly informant's mind; it demonstrates what becomes of the oral tradition of a group undergoing rapid European acculturation. It is possible, nonetheless, to question the choice of words like "thither" and "thence." To the modern reader, at least, they smack of an affected diction. In this text they seem rather incongruous (in terms of associations with other English works they suggest) with the colloquial sharpness of "Say, what are you doing?" or "You caught us swimming in the lake our father owns. Come, give me my skin." They also pose the question of what the corresponding Haida terms would be. Ideally, in Haida they would not only be approximate in meaning, but would hold similar associations for Haida as words belonging to a stylized, somewhat "literary" diction. This problem of translation, as part of the whole difficulty of comprehending any literature in translation, has been studied by I. A. Richards. It is a difficulty commonly recognized by anthropologists. Richards writes,

> . . . can we maintain two systems of thinking in our minds without reciprocal infection and yet in some way mediate between them? And does not such mediation require yet a third system of thought general enough and comprehensive enough to include them both? And how are we to prevent this third system from being only our own familiar, established, tradition of thinking rigged out in some fresh terminology or other disguise?[33]

The answer—or rather attitude—that Richards proposes is that of "Multiple Definition"—

> It is a proposal for a systematic survey of the language we are forced to use in translation, of the ranges of possible meanings which may be carried both by our chief pivotal terms—such as Knowledge, Truth, Order, Nature, Principle, Thought, Feeling, Mind, Datum, Law, Reason. . . .[34]

In short, the total meaning of a word, "of which Intention, Feeling, Tone, and Sense seem to be the main components."[35] These problems belong in the realm of Semantics and are to be differentiated from specific difficulties attached to the workings of the Haida language. They include another possibility which is simply that in languages of cultures which have not developed a highly analytic, discursive mode of thinking, the words are more connotative—and approach the nature of metaphoric or "mythical" images rather than denotative terms. The action of this connotative content puts the language in more direct relation to the other aspects of culture. According to Malinowski:

> . . . language is essentially rooted in the reality of a culture, the tribal life and customs of a people, and . . . it cannot be explained without constant reference to these broader contexts of verbal utterance.[36]

This use of language is described by Richards as the "emotive" use, as opposed to "scientific" use:

> The distinction once clearly grasped is simple. We may either use words for the sake of the references they promote, or we may use them for the sake of the attitudes and emotions which ensue.[37]

Literature exploits the emotive possibilities of language, and is to be evaluated in terms of how well the possibilities in the language are utilized—as technical skill—which is equivalent to evoking an organized, complex, and satisfactory emotional response in the reader. All primitive speech is closer to literature or "poetry" than is realized, if one accepts this view. The translator is faced with a range of emotive-associational potentialities in each word which cannot exist in his own language, and the purely referential translation he must be satisfied with is a sterile formula compared to the richness of the original.

This text, if one pares down the terms which are no longer effective in English literature, and straightens out the pronouns (there are several passages in which pronoun references become highly confusing), gives promise of being a brief, but complete narrative, which is capable of evoking a surprisingly rich body of associations, and in human content presents a highly charged situation. The text falls neatly into the archetypal divisions of marriage, loss, quest, and reunion. If one is not overly disturbed by the hero's untimely end—which might even contribute to the merit of the myth for some readers—the story resolves in a perplexing, but emotionally potent manner. Even as it stands, there are good lines in it. Many sentences fall naturally into a predominantly anapestic rhythmic pattern:

> The roots of their tales were spotted with white.
>
> He entered his father's house with her.
>
> She went to the place where her skin was kept.
>
> She was eating the stalks of the sea grass which grew there.
>
> Then he entered his silver salmon skin and swam up to
>   meet him

It is possible to cite more. These examples also bring out the "fairy-tale" tone of the piece—another factor in the English-speaking reader's response. In terms of the associations English-speaking readers are apt to make, there is more chance of its being received sympathetically today than thirty years ago. The works of Joyce, Eliot, Mann, Kafka, and others, often consciously patterned on myths, have accustomed modern readers to unexpected transformations and radical, symbolic situations. The narrative has suggestions of unspoken meanings—underlying relationships established by the hero and other characters which are not explicit to the reader. The sudden appearance of goose girls in a lake close to the town; a wife that merely smells human food and makes completely inexplicable nightly journeys to eat shore grass where "As the waves broke in they moved her shore-ward" could be invested with sinister or sublime allegorical meanings. The formalized—one is almost tempted to say ritualized—nature of the hero's quest (unlike so many European Swan-Maiden tales) is puzzling insofar as complete understanding seems to exist between the characters. There is no questioning of motives. The old man at the end of town, the apparently aimless, timeless beings he meets on his journey, all are acquainted with his task and know, as he does, precisely what must be done. It is only a matter of fulfilling the already understood. The repetition of "brave man" as epithet is also ambiguous, and almost sounds given in a spirit of irony. "Now, brave man, go on. The trail runs inland behind my house." The Mouse Woman, briefly as she appears, is given a personality: "Then he took her by the back with his fingers and put her across. Her tail was bent up between her ears for joy. . . ." "Her voice sounded sharp" and the unexpected "I will lend you what I wore when I went hunting when I was young." These faintly humorous statements are suggestive of a possible extension of meaning and association in the myth which the sentences are only signposts to. One of the most confusing points is reached when the hero elaborately tricks Master Hopper and the firewood-chopping men to gain knowledge which they were prepared with in advance. They tell him most casually, "This house is your wife's." The basic human content of the myth—the winning, loss, and regaining of love—provides it with an immediate interest to all readers. The unclear motivations, and the succession of sharp imagelike incidents remove it from the realm of popular romance, which could never have a hero undergo a series of tasks for his beloved (winning the Football Game, getting the job as Jr. Exec. at the Advertising Agency), achieve the happy reunion, only to end with, "After he had been there for some time he came to dislike the place." The Haida Swan-Maiden myth may be closer to life, and in its remote and suggested meanings, closer to the archetype as well. If the archetype's significance is real—as Jung argues—we are not only delighted by the bizarre tone, the sudden, explosive dialogue, and the sharp contrasts of indefiniteness and concrete statement, but stirred to the depths of our psychological being. As Campbell might phrase it, this manifestation of a primal meaning—after having been lost (in this particular version's history) to Western civilization for centuries and swept through untold tribes and languages, has reappeared in a Government Bulletin to take its place humbly alongside the Arthurian romances, the *Divine Comedy, The Waste Land,* and *The Rime of the Ancient Mariner* as a slight, but complete, version of the Theme.

5. ARCHETYPES AND VERSIONS

To justify the study of motifs, types, and archetypes on a comparative basis as relevant to the investigation of a single version, some linkage between the stylistic nature of the archetype and the publicly recited oral tale must be established. The only place where such linkage could effectively shape narrative would be in the mind of the artist. It is possible to make a series of connections on the basis of psychological generalizations which may indicate that such a process actually operates.

Radin's category of "thinkers," as has been noted, includes poet, priest, and shaman. The shaman has been distinguished from the priest as functioning within a religious framework requiring individual spirit possession. In trances, he experiences dream visions, and often inflicts considerable pain on himself. Radin is no Jungian and is aggresively anti-psychological, but in his description of the shaman's activity, he is forced to psychologize:

> Pain and suffering (for the shaman) . . . was the expression of a conflict within himself, the splitting off of an unconscious state from a conscious one and its subsequent reintegration on a new level of awareness. This synthesis was then projected outward and re-enacted before the world as the drama of man's perpetual struggle for security, a security to which he attains by delving into the unknown and by becoming as one with the hidden and mysterious.[38]

The nature of the shaman's trance, and the dream journey he takes while possessed by spirits, is described by Campbell as noted among the Altai:

> On his laborious journey, reports another observer, "The shaman has to encounter and master a number of differing obstacles (pudak) which are not always easily overcome. After he has wandered through dark forests and over massive ranges of mountains, where he occasionally comes across the bones of other shamans and their animal mounts who have died along the way, he reaches an opening in the ground. The most difficult stages of the journey now begin, when the depths of the underworld with their remarkable manifestations open before him. . . . After he has appeased the watchers of the kingdom of the dead and made his way past the numerous perils, he comes at last to the Lord of the Underworld, Erlik himself. And the latter rushes against him, horribly bellowing; but if the shaman is sufficiently skillful, he can sooth the monster back again with promises of luxurious offerings. This moment of the dialogue with Erlik is the crisis of the ceremonial. The shaman passes into an ecstasy.[39]

This publicly observed trance of the shaman is "simply making both visible and public the systems of symbolic fantasy that are present in the psyche of every adult member of their society"[40] and is a manifestation of the archetypal images, as may be seen in the quest-nature of the shaman's dream. The individual who experiences this, and the priests and artists who potentially would experience it in a society which demanded it, fall into Jung's introvert category. Such individuals experience an intensity of inner life which even today is characteristic of the poet's experience. According to Richards, the poet is

> . . . pre-eminently accessible to external influences and discriminating with regard to them. . . . The greatest difference between the artist or poet and the ordinary person is found, as has often been pointed out, in the range, delicacy, and the freedom of the connections he is able to make between the different elements of his experience.[41]

Because of this availability to experience he may appear a "mental chaos"—yet his inner organization will receive and control diverse experiences, and recast them in symbolic form.[42]

Omitting some of the steps in this argument, the conclusion one is led to is that the best narrators in primitive society are the individuals most apt to be unconsciously influenced by the type of inner experience which Jung describes as the assertion of archetypal principles and images. These individuals may even be trained to undergo dream and trance states which, according to Jung, bring the basic imagery to the fore. If this possibility is admitted, it is easy to see how an occasional brilliant and "available" narrator would experience the archetypal significance and keep it alive in his retelling of myths. Similarly, there would be individuals in his audience for whom it would operate on more than narrative level. Thus, the study of the archetype will indicate the nature of a symbolic framework which we can expect to find embedded in the best individual myths and tales because highly receptive individuals have put and kept it there.

If one rejects the Jungian significance of the archetype, another linkage is possible, more tenuous in its way, but perhaps more respectable scientifically. This is the stylistic nature of archetypal material, and its metaphorical relation to the actual world. This aspect will require Sapir's form-libido social psychology—yet unborn—to describe the processes which must take place somewhere between the observable fact of a multitude of versions, and the inducible fact of a limited number of types. A few attempts at explaining it as a function of symbolic form have been attempted. Hermann Broch argues a language-transcending stylistic force in myths, particularly in the archetypal structures, that enables them to survive through time. He terms this "The style of old age"—claiming that "myth embraces qualities both . . . of childhood . . . and that of old age, the styles of both expressing the essential and nothing but the essential. . . ."[43] More concretely, he describes it as

> . . . a kind of abstractism in which the expression relies less and less on the vocabulary, which finally becomes reduced to a few prime symbols, and instead relies more and more on the syntax: for in essence this is what abstractism is—the impoverishment of vocabulary and the enrichment of the syntactical relations of expression. . . . In the complicated interplay between vocabulary and syntax, as it appears in the arts, most of the vocables are the result of syntactical combinations which become universally accepted conventions, i.e., as symbols, and as such are regarded as naturalistic representations.[44]

In these terms, knowledge of the archetype is knowledge of a set of relationships between variable images, and these relationships are so much a part of any narrative that for the myth or tale to maintain its identity in transmission, the narrative must continue to contain the underlying relationships—which act on the material which fills in the framework (words, images, attitudes) of the total version in a partially determining fashion. The relationships are created and recurrent in the first place because of man's need to "build perceptive models of the world" and myth becomes an "abbreviation of the world content by presenting its structure, and this in its very essence.[45]

In a similar argument, Northrop Frye has proposed that

> . . . the literary anthropologist who chases the source of the Hamlet legend from the pre-Shakespeare play to Saxo, and from Saxo to nature myths, is not running away from Shakespeare: he is drawing closer to the archetypal form which Shakespeare recreated.[46]

This is because the archetype is structurally basic to the elaborated work. The scholar must know it in its pure form to have a standard of comparison against which the complete work of art (version) may be seen as a true, perceptive, and technically skillful development of the basic structural relationships, or as an incomplete utilization—indicating a faulty formal sense, or carelessness, in the artist—and producing an incompletely controlled literary product. The artist must be true to the requirements of his culture, and the requirements of his Theme as Form, to produce a version in which topical and universal significance are fused. This fusion is one of the requirements of the greatest and most enduring literary works—Homer being, perhaps, the prime example. In the Haida story the process may also be seen. Like the figure in Hugh Vereker's carpet, the archetypal form

> . . . stretches from book to book, and everything else, comparatively, plays over the surface of it. . . . It's stuck into every volume as your foot is stuck into your shoe. It governs every line, it chooses every word, and it dots every i, it places every comma.[47]

CHAPTER VI

FUNCTION OF THE MYTH

1. INTRODUCTORY

Contemporary theory of the function of mythology almost inevitably involves theory of the function of language, ritual, religion, and art—either as similar but separate modes of psychocultural activity, or as ultimately identical aspects of the same thing, sometimes termed "Myth" in the broader sense of all symbolic cognition. The philosophical substructures implied in most of these theories include everything from metaphysics to theory of knowledge. In utilizing concepts from them it will be impossible to take into account the possible criticisms of their basic assumptions. My intention is to present the possible extent of the cultural function of the Haida Swan-Maiden myth, through a description and discussion of general statements by individuals of philosophical, literary, psychological, and anthropological persuasions. In doing so it may be argued that I am misinterpreting a theory or ignoring some underlying assumptions.

I can only answer that the total view achieved by this me method is my own doing, created by the selection of relevant concepts and implying no criticism of or assent to, any one point of view. It may appear, through my manner of presentation, that the scholars quoted are all in essential agreement. This is, to the best of my knowledge, only occasionally true, and under the peaceful surface of this discussion rage a number of minor controversies with which I am but superficially acquainted.

Anthropological studies dealing with oral literature as a functional element in culture are rare; and they are, with few exceptions, restricted to generalizing on the subject of mythology. Functionally oriented ethnology has never been practiced on the Haida. The concluding definition of the Haida Swan-Maiden myth will be the product of the most speculative approach in this thesis. Its verification would require residence in the culture, which for me is not possible.

The basic assumption of this chapter is that mythology has a function in culture. This may seem too obvious a fact to require statement, but many past theories of mythology have operated as if myths were irrational diseases from which savage minds suffered, or the result of idle, mistaken savage speculation in which elaborate stories were constructed to describe the phases of the moon or processes of sunrise and sunset. Much of the modern interest in mythology stems from the recognition of its social function, as does the even more recent attitude of some scholars and poets that the function mythology serves in primitive culture is desperately needed by contemporary society. The progress-minded nineteenth-century anthropologists, for whom mythology seemed curious, irrational, and "wrong," could never have discovered the world-shaking significance in irrational and (to Andrew Lang's continual dismay) sometimes bestial little stories which today are seen as descriptions of man's inmost needs. For example, take the modern associations attached to the Oedipus myth.

This chapter will first present statements of the function and nature of mythology, then clarify the sociopsychological processes as studied by Abram Kardiner, link together a number of other views on the function of mythology in his terms, and conclude with a summary of the entire thesis and the dimensions of mythology as indicated by this study.

2. DESCRIPTION OF THE FUNCTION

Recognition of the social function of mythology may be traced, in terms of the first influential, articulate public statement on the subject, to Bronislaw Malinowski's "Myth in Primitive Psychology," published in 1926.[1] His essay was based on field observation among the Trobriand Islanders. He wrote:

> Myth as it exists in a savage community, that is, in its living primitive form, is not merely a story told but a reality lived. It is not of the nature of fiction, such as we read today in a novel, but it is a living reality, believed to have once happened in primeval times, and continuing ever since to influence the world and human destinies. This myth is to the savage what, to a fully believing Christian, is the Biblical story of Creation, of the Fall, of the Redemption by Christ's Sacrifice on the Cross. As our sacred story lives in our ritual, in our morality, as it governs our faith and controls our conduct, even so does his myth for the savage.[2]
>
> . . . Myth fulfills in primitive culture an indispensable function: it expresses, enhances, and codifies belief; it safeguards and enforces morality; it vouches for the efficiency of ritual and contains practical rules for the guidance of man. Myth is thus a vital ingredient of human civilization; it is not an idle tale, but a hard-worked active force; it is not an intellectual explanation or an artistic imagery, but a pragmatic character of primitive faith and moral wisdom.[3]

Although Malinowski's essay, which was limited to primitve culture, emphasized the necessity of studying mythology in the cultural context, he has been cited by later writers with divergent and much more inclusive views of myth. Mark Schorer, for example:

> Myths are the instruments by which we continually struggle to make our experience intelligible to ourselves. A myth is a large, controlling image that gives philosophical meaning to the facts of ordinary life; that is, which has organizing value for experience.[4]

> . . . Literature ceases to be perceptual and tends to degenerate into mere description without adequate myth; for, to cite Malinowski, myth, continually modified and renewed by the modification of history, is in some form an "indispensable ingredient of all culture."[5]

On the same page Schorer quotes Jung, and shows indebtedness to Jung's view of myth by the statement "Myth is fundamental, the dramatic representation of our deepest instinctual life."

The same essay provoked an objection from Robert Lowie:

> . . . What if myth is "not merely a story but a reality lived?" We cannot relive the reality, but we can study that textual rendering which Malinowski disdains as merely the "intellectual" aspect of the tales divorced from their mystic aura.[6]

C. Kerenyi made the complete marriage of Malinowski's view and Jungian theory, while setting out to show that we *can* relive the reality. He quotes the entire "reality lived" passage and writes:

> The myth, he (Malinowski) says, is not an explanation put forward to satisfy scientific curiosity; it is the re-arising of a primordial reality in narrative form.[7]

> Mythology gives a ground, lays a foundation. It does not answer the question "why," but "whence?" In Greek we can put this difference very nicely. Mythology does not actually indicate "causes," *aitia*. It does this (is "aetiological") only to the extent that . . . the *aitia* are *archai* or first principles . . . (hap-

penings in mythology) are the *archai* to which everything individual and particular goes back and out of which it is made, whilst they remain ageless, inexhaustible, invincible in timeless primordiality, in a past that proves imperishable because of its eternally repeated rebirths.[8]

Kerenyi suggests the possibility of the archetypal "mythologems" being present—literally—in the physical beginnings of man:

> He experiences it (the mythologem) as his own absolute *archai*, a beginning since when he was a unity fusing in itself all the contradictions of his nature and life to be. To this origin, understood as the beginning of a new world-unity, the mythologem of the *divine child* points. The mythologem of the *maiden goddess* points to yet another *archai*, also experienced as one's own origin but which is at the same time the *archai* of countless beings before and after oneself, and by virtue of which the individual is endowed with infinity already in the germ.[9]

Another scholar who is well aware of Malinowski's work is I. A. Richards. He wrote of the "greater and saner mythologies"—

> They are no amusement or diversion to be sought as a relaxation and an escape from the hard realities of life. They are these hard realities in projection, their symbolic recognition, coordination and acceptance. Through such mythologies our will is collected, our powers unified, our growth controlled. . . . Without his mythologies man is only a cruel animal without a soul—for a soul is a central part of his governing mythology—he is a congeries of possibilities without order and without aim.[10]

Kerenyi's theory remains so problematical as to render no heuristic service. Of Schorer's and Richards' views—if they are to prove of value—we must ask: how and why are hard realities projected, and how, once projected, do they serve as "controlling images"—and what do they control? The two key words "projection" and "control" have been used before in this essay in connection with the cultural content of mythology, and the operation of magic and ritual. The investigation of these words will show them to mean essentially the same thing in the various contexts cited, and demonstrate what Malinowski probably had in mind when he said that a myth is a reality lived.

3. KARDINER'S USE OF THE TERM "PROJECTION"

Abram Kardiner uses the term "projection" in a fairly specific sense, and in doing so describes what he conceives the process to be psychologically—and how values get into myths. His psychology is a socially-oriented neo-Freudianism. In *The Individual and His Society*[11] and *The Psychological Frontiers of Society*[12] he has presented a method of study and interpretation of culture which he believes will enable the student to determine the formative institutions (those institutions which regulate the formative experiences of childhood) and the influences of these institutions on the individual personality and total cultural configuration. The analysis of the mythology of the culture under observation plays an important part in Kardiner's analysis:

> We have had up to this point a series of inferences about the probable effects of certain formative institutions. How can this guess be substantiated or contradicted? If your hypothesis is correct, namely that these conditions in childhood become consolidated and form a basis for subsequent projective use, then we can expect to find some evidence of it in all projective systems . . . religious, folklore, and perhaps other institutions. In other words, if we know how the basic personality is established, we can make certain predictions about the institutions this personality is likely to invent. If we follow the particular personality created by the above mentioned conditions (sporadic minimal parental care, teasing of and deliberate misrepresentation to, children by parents) we expect to find folk tales dealing with parental hatred, with desertion by parents. . . .[13]

Kardiner's assumption is that as the individual personality is shaped by the primary institutions, the oral prose-narrative, possessed and transmitted by the group, will mirror a group-personality derived from childhood experience. In reversing the process, he believes the culture's basic personality will reflect the psychologically relevant elements to be found in the tales. Kardiner's technique in both books is to cite ethnographic material on a culture, including a selection of abstracted tales, then to analyze the culture on the basis of the ethnographer's report and his own psychological assumptions, and finally, to cite the folktales as corroborative evidence of the truth of his analysis. In doing so, he avoids any discussion of the world distribution of types and motifs involved. The primary institutions center in the family structure—maternal care, induction of affectivity, maternal attitudes, early disciplines, sexual disciplines and institutionalized sibling attitudes. He lists these and a number of other institutions as the "Key Integrative Systems" which he ranks in terms of their manifestation in the basic personality structure as follows:

1. Projective systems based on experience with the aid of rationalizations, generalizations, systematization and elaboration. To this category belong the security system of the individual and the superego systems, that is, those dealing with conscience and ideals.
2. Learned systems connected with drives.
3. Learned systems in which no drives are involved but ideas associated with activities. Groups 2 and 3 lay the basis for specific psychosomatic tension release routes.
4. Taboo systems, all learned as part of reality.
5. Pure empirical reality systems, subject to demonstrations.
6. Value systems and ideologies (which cut across all previous systems.)[14]

Projective systems are schematically represented by Kardiner as being created in the following manner:

Nuclear experiences which define apperceptions and emotionally directed interests, e.g., punishments for delinquency.

(resulting in:)

> Abstraction and generalization: e.g., "If I am obedient I will suffer no pain."

(resulting in:)

> Projection and systematization: e.g., "I am ill, therefore I have wronged."

(resulting in:)

> Rationalization (equals) ideology (equals) a system to overcome tensions:
> "There is a supreme being who observes my behavior. He has the attributes of omnipotence and omniscience, etc. If I do wrong I will be punished. If I suffer I will be reinstated." Once this system is accepted as reality, any number of rational systems can be devised to "prove" it, to modify it, or to render it workable.[15]

By the same process a body of mythology is created, although the projected attitudes are contained in narrative form. In his analysis of Comanche folklore, for instance, Kardiner finds these underlying projections:

> The story of the faithless wife who sides with the Ute against her husband and is punished by him is another evidence of the underlying distrust of women, undoubtedly a projection of their (the Comanches') own anxiety about loss of power for war and sex alike.

A magic-flight story of children (Hansel and Gretel type):

> It belittles the importance of parental care, and in sour-grapes fashion indicates that they (the children) don't need the parents anyway, they can look after themselves. This seems very like a protest against the unusual burdens placed on the child to emulate the parents and to become prematurely independent.[16]

Kardiner divides the integrational systems into the major categories of "reality" and "projective" systems. He writes:

> In every society studied we found evidence of these two systems. The empirical reality systems were found in the manipu-

lation and making of tools, the knowledge of planting, and so forth; the projective systems in religion, folklore, and many other systems.

> These two types of mental process depend upon different orders of experience. . . . Both have emotional components . . . the experiential base of a projective system is generally forgotten; its only remains in the personality are to be found in the conditioned perceptions. . . . Projective systems are . . . excrescences developed from nuclear traumatic experiences within the growth pattern of the individual.[17]

He terms the latter system the "projective screen"—and in his discussion of its operation, becomes so annoyed with it as to ignore its functional value:

> The fantasy or projective screen hides social realities, and one cannot come to grips with them because the fantasy screen itself becomes the chief object of preoccupation and is mistaken for the reality to be dealt with.[18]

In the same chapter, he admits "there is no difference between the actual logical or ratiocinative processes in the two (reality and projective) systems."[19] The projective screen appears to be identical with what writers term "Myth" in its broadest sense: the Myth that reflects projected values, and in doing so reinforces the social fabric individual by individual, making it possible for the culture to survive. In admitting the identity of mental processes in the two systems, Kardiner lays himself open to the charge of projecting Western values in assuming that there are any "social realities" actually masked by the projective screen. For the culture in question, mythological and social realities are identical, and the function of mythology is to enforce this fusion—even though, to use Richards' term, the projections are of "hard realities." An even more extreme attack on Kardiner's dichotomy between projective and reality systems could be made from the philosophical stand denying the dualism of subject and object: the whole world is a projection, and mythology a particularly ordered projection which enables the more chaotic aspects of the world to be classified and comprehended.

Whether one agrees with Kardiner's projective-reality dichotomy or not, the careful scholarship and documented arguments of the two books, particularly the later one, are extremely convincing. Kardiner's description of the nature of projection undoubtedly covers a number of its most basic aspects and provides, if one accepts the Freudian tenets, a very workable theory of the interrelations of culture, personality, and mythology.

4. PROJECTION AND CONTROL

The ideas, attitudes, or situations projected into a myth— those derived from everyday experience as well as the less obvious ones based on childhood experience—have a peculiar relationship with the symbolic units representing them in narrative. The social value and the values expressed in myth are somehow connected, and in the myth's function, the projected unit appears to control and shape the experiences it was derived from, rather than remaining a subsidiary reflection of experience. Wherever mythology functions as a living part of culture, this may generally be said to be true. It is a fact of great significance about the human mind, and it has puzzled and annoyed rational-minded thinkers from the beginnings of Western philosophy right up to Kardiner. The myth unit does not control by any physical means, however, but by a metaphorical similarity to experience: by a process of sympathetic magic.

The identification of the operation of mythical narrative for the group with the principles of sympathetic magic —through the association of images with acts, causing the culture to take the image as primary to the act, and then to organize the acts in accordance with the myth, seems less farfetched when the close relationships between ritual and myths are recalled. Ritual is a conscious, community-enacted drama—often based on mythical plots and portraying characters from mythology—designed to control certain natural forces by enacting metaphorically similar situations in which the desired results are symbolically attained. Ritual unites the group and individual consciousness in a sense of community that not only breaks down the distinction between the two psychologically, but enforces the identity of projective and physical reality so as to make the whole universe become an aspect of the human community.[20] Individual acts of magic operate in a similar fashion, taking place within the larger framework of belief. The whole "religious control of the universe" derives its potency from sympathetic, not physical actions on things. Sympathetic magic is, as Frazer points out, based on "mistaken" associations, and never actually shapes physical events. Functionally, however, it is a real force, and literally controls human affairs. It never controls them according to principles that run counter to physical fact in nature—part of the efficacy of the projective screen is its close integration with physical laws which concern the economic survival of the group. On the basis of this fact, Campbell writes,

> It has been customary to describe the seasonal festivals of so-called native peoples as efforts to control nature. This is a misrepresentation. There is much of the will to control in every act of man . . . (but) . . . the dominant motive in all truly religious (as opposed to black-magical) ceremonial is that of submission to the inevitables of destiny—and in the seasonal festivals this motive is particularly apparent.
>
> No tribal rite has yet been recorded which attempts to keep winter from descending; on the contrary, all rites prepare the community to endure, together with the rest of nature, the season of the terrible cold. And in the spring, the rites do not seek to compel nature to pour forth immediately corn, beans, and squash for the lean community; on the contrary: the rites dedicate the whole people to the work of nature's season.[21]

Myth is, functionally, the verbal equivalent of ritual, magically operating with words, images, and situations in narrative form as ritual operates with symbolic acts.

Each of the narrative levels in a myth is capable of working as sympathetic magic, so that the complex of symbol-referent equivalences that may be found in any one myth in principle is a hierarchy (proceeding from particulars to wholes) of symbolic modes which is, at its farthest extent, culture itself. To clarify this, Frazer's description of the magical function of words must be recalled:

> Unable to discriminate clearly between words and things, the savage commonly fancies that the link between a name and the person or thing denominated by it is not a mere arbitrary and ideal association, but a real and substantial bond which unites the two in such a way that magic may be wrought on a man just as easily through his name as through his hair, his nails, or any other material part of his person.[22]

This is elaborated by Malinowski, who based his discussion on field observation:

> . . . we are made to realize how deeply rooted is the belief that a word has some power over a thing, that it is akin or even identical in its contained "meaning" with the thing or with its prototype. . . . The word gives power, allows one to exercise an influence over an object or an action. . . . . The word acts on the thing and the thing releases the word in the human mind. This indeed is nothing more or less than the essence of the theory which underlies the use of verbal magic.[23]

Language and myth both derive from these principles, and although they become divergent at later "stages," the underlying relationship may always be seen, according to Ernst Cassirer:

> . . . for, no matter how widely the contents of myth and language may differ, yet the same form of mental conception is operative in both. It is the form which one may denote as *metaphorical thinking.*[24]

Metaphorical thinking is the subjective identification of symbols and referents—on the basis of the control of symbol over referent—in Cassirer's view; another way of saying sympathetic magic.

Language, it is sometimes argued, is a fundamental prerequisite of ideation. Although this point cannot be adequately proved or refuted, it is certain A. L. Kroeber is right in assuming the necessity of language for the existence of culture:

> Cultural activity, even of the simplest kind, inevitably rests on ideas or generalizations; and such or any ideas, in turn, human minds seem to be able to formulate and operate with and transmit only through speech. Nature consists of an endless array of particular phenomena. To combine these particulars into a generalization or an abstraction, such as passing from potential awareness of the thousands of stones along a river bed into the idea of stone as a distinctive material—this synthesis appears to require production of some kind of symbol, perhaps as a sort of psychological catalyzing agent: a symbol such as the sounds that make up the word *stone*. In short, culture can probably function only on the basis of abstractions, and these in turn seem to be possible only through speech.[25]

As the single word abstracts and controls for the user the essence of its referent; the image, metaphor, and myth abstract, organize, and symbolically represent larger blocks of experience—patterns of experience—which can be psychologically controlled by the individual because of their essential compact form. Actual experience is too disorganized and chaotic to allow the individual or group any feeling of security and order without the myth mechanism. In culture, language is a learned function which almost always communicates over any length of time within patterns of verbal significance larger than particular words. Mythology is the central patterning force of that verbal organization which survives through generations, containing the cosmology and value-system of the group. Even if the mythology is, as Kardiner says, ultimately the product of certain human institutions—the survival of the institutions in culture depends on the continuation of the mythological function. Myth is a "reality lived" because for every individual it contains, at the moment of telling, the projected content of both his unarticulated and conscious values: simultaneously ordering, organizing, and making comprehensible the world within which the values exist. One might even reformulate the statement to say "Reality is a myth lived."

The mythological symbolizing of experience, and the subsequent control of experience, has been seen by some writers as the principle of any organization of value and knowledge. A comparatively early statement of this view was that of George Santayana:

> Mythology and theology are the most striking illustrations of this human method of incorporating much diffuse experience into graphic and picturesque ideas; but steady reflection will hardly allow us to see anything else in the theories of science and philosophy.[26]

This attitude toward the projective screen of "Myth" is common today among literary critics and a few philosophers. Susanne Langer's *Philosophy in a New Key*[27] relates the nature and function of mythology and ritual to a fundamental symbol-making activity of man, basic to his nature. She states the relation of this theory to modern science:

> The problem of observation is all but eclipsed by the problem of *meaning*. And the truth of empiricism in science is jeopardized by the surprising truth that our sense-data are primarily symbols.[28]

Individuals create their private symbolisms, and as the private symbolisms become articulately expressed in some cultures—particularly those with writing—complicated interactions of individual and group mythologies

> . . . in a never ending interplay of symbolic gestures, built up the pyramided structure called civilization. In this structure very few bricks touch the ground.[29]

The function of mythology may then be summarized: it provides a symbolic representation of projected values and empirical knowledge within a framework of belief which relates individual, group, and physical environment, to the end of integration and survival. The implication of this function for modern literary theory has been seized by many critics. For example:

> Our view . . . sees the meaning and function of literature as centrally present in metaphor and myth.[30]

Or T. S. Eliot's discussion of the use of the *Odyssey* by James Joyce as an ordering framework for his novel *Ulysses*:

> In using the myth, in manipulating a continuous parallel between contemporaneity and antiquity, Mr. Joyce is pursuing a method which others must pursue after him. They will not be imitators, any more than the scientist who uses the discoveries of an Einstein in pursuing his own, independent, further investigations. It is simply a way of controlling, of ordering, of giving a shape and a significance to the immense panorama of futility and anarchy which is contemporary history. . . . Psychology (such as it is, and whether our reaction to it be comic or serious), ethnology, and *The Golden Bough* have concurred to make what was impossible even a few years ago. Instead of narrative method, we may now use the mythical method.[31]

One of the most extreme statements by a contemporary literary critic is that of Philip Wheelwright, who sees the community myth-consciousness as essential for good literature—

> The poetry of our time doesn't matter much, it is a last echo of something important that was alive long ago. What matters is the myth-consciousness of the next generations, the spiritual seed that we plant in our children; their loves and insights and incubating sense of significant community. On that depend the possibilities of future greatness—in poetry and everything else.[32]

A number of contemporary poets are not giving up yet, however. Some, like Robert Graves and Peter Viereck, have taken to speaking of the "magical" nature of poetry. Viereck sees no contradiction in his insistence on both "classicism" in poetry and its "holy dread"—the two formulate a

> . . . dualism of what Nietzsche called the Dionysian and Apollonian; also the "dark gods" of the unconscious and the more rational, civilized conscious mind. The creative tension of these antitheses is in the shiver of holy dread, the tragic exaltation which makes the hair stand on end and is the difference between poetry and verse.[33]

He refers to the "all-important night-side of art, its magic" much as Graves claims,

> Poetry began in the matriarchal age, and derives its magic from the moon, not from the sun. No poet can hope to understand the nature of poetry unless he has had a vision of the Naked King crucified to the lopped oak, and watched the dancers, red-eyed from the acrid smoke of the sacrificial fires, stamping out the measure of the dance, their bodies bent uncouthly forward, with a monotonous chant of: "Kill! kill! kill!" and "Blood! blood! blood!"[34]

The literary interest in magic derives from three sources: Frazer's *The Golden Bough*, Malinowski's *Myth in Primitive Psychology*, and Jung's *Psychology of the Unconscious*. Frazer presented the theory of magic and the concrete symbols attached to the strangely memorable myths of the dying god; Malinowski described the function of myth, and Jung suggested the possibility that it might be possible to write literature using symbols from Frazer which would function in modern civilization—for individuals—as myth functions in primitive culture for the group. In doing so, the poet would not only be creating workable private mythologies for his readers, but moving toward the formation of a new social mythology. This is the duty of the modern artist, according to Campbell, who believes that only in the "storehouse of recorded values"—literature—can this be accomplished:

It is not society that is to guide and save the creative hero, but precisely the reverse. And so every one of us shares the supreme ordeal—carries the cross of the redeemer—not in the bright moments of his tribe's great victories, but in the silences of his personal despair.[35]

It is impossible to test the function of the Haida Swan-Maiden myth against such inclusive theorizing. It is important to repeat, nonetheless, that the Swan-Maiden story was a myth, not a tale, among the Haida. An element of belief was present. The myth undoubtedly had some function—not very important, perhaps, since it is merely a very short myth and not the whole mythology. It played an inconspicuous role among the longer, more important myths of the Raven cycle, probably serving as entertainment during potlatches and the long winter ceremonials. It must be remembered that this is no mean role: the potlatch, as described in chapter two, was one of the key institutions of the Haida, enabling the prestige and class system to reassert itself periodically, and providing a social situation in which the reciting of myths was required. As one of these myths, the Swan-Maiden story was at the center of Haida life. It reinforced the Haida conception of the universe, of the nature of supernatural beings and animals, and of the nature of human intercourse with the supernatural sphere. Many large, important works of literature in the Western canon do proportionately less in relation to the values of their culture.

5. CONCLUSION

The dimensions of the myth: The myth has been seen as social document, as the product of historical diffusion and compounded from motifs distributed all over the world, as metaphysical and psychological truth in symbolic form, as literature, and as a vital functioning aspect of a culture. The fact that a myth is many things at once is obvious, but the specialists in each of the many realms of knowledge I have drawn from do not communicate much with each other. For that reason, in almost any single-approach study of mythology it is always possible to find statements which a specialist from another field could easily refute.

The dimensions of the approaches: The problems of mythology cut across the boundaries of scholarly disciplines —and no one approach can hope to do justice to the many ways in which any myth is related to (1) its culture, (2) the body of world mythology, (3) culture as an abstract universal, (4) the working of the human mind and the values it sets up. In its totality the study of a myth is the study of "man and his works."

The thorough investigation: such inclusiveness is neither possible or desirable in the work of individual scholars. One can ask which aspect of the study of mythology should the student concerned with oral literature consider central to an investigation which would take into account the many factors suggested in this thesis, yet not lose itself in theoretical ramifications which do not illuminate oral literature itself. The answer, I believe, must be the individual version. Working with a single version, complete with language and culture attached, will keep one continually referring back to the social existence of the myth or tale, even while pursuing the fascinating but occasionally fanciful possibilities it may possess. Within any single version, as this study has suggested, there is a richness of process and significance that remains important—no matter how slight the version and how marginal the culture—to all human activity. Concrete insights derived from the study of individual versions, rare as they are in present-day studies, will surely prove useful to the understanding of the imaginative and social life of man. I have not unearthed any particular insights of this order, but perhaps I have shown why one may validly point to even "He Who Hunted Birds in His Father's Village" and say, "There digge!"

CHAPTER I: THE MYTH

1   This is the complete text as recorded by John Swanton and interpreted by Henry Moody in "Haida Texts and Myths," *Bureau of American Ethnology Bulletin* 29 (1905), p. 264.

2   As was once customary with the sons of chiefs. (Swanton's note)

3   Canada geese. (Swanton's note)

4   Plants with edible roots growing around the mouths of creeks. (Swanton's note) I have changed Indian names throughout this study, from phonetic spelling to their nearest English equivalents.

5   Such as were used to make awls and gimlets out of. (Swanton's note)

6   Supernatural beings are often said to be tickled by having someone merely look at them. (Swanton's note)

7   This is undoubtedly the pole held on the breast of Supernatural-being-standing-and-moving, which rose in the middle of the

Haida country and extended to the sky. (Swanton's note)

8 Master Hopper (*Lkienqa-ixon*), referred to in many other places throughout these stories. He was a one-legged supernatural being, or a supernatural being having one leg shorter than the other. Here he is represented as only a half-man. (Swanton's note)

9 That is, the man became a seagull. (Swanton's note)

CHAPTER II: THE MYTH AND THE CULTURE

1 Franz Boas, "The Mythology and Folktales of the North American Indians" (1914) in *Race, Language, and Culture* (New York: Macmillan 1949, copyright 1940), p. 463.

2 Ibid., p. 476.

3 P. E. Goddard, *Indians of the Northwest Coast* (American Museum of Natural History Handbooks, 1924), p. 16.

4 Ibid., p. 19.

5 Ibid.

6 Franz Boas, "Tsimshian Mythology," *Thirty-first Report of the Bureau of American Ethnology* (1909-10), p. 46.

7 Clark Wissler, *The American Indian* (New York: Oxford, 1933), p. 229.

8 A. L. Kroeber, "American Culture and the Northwest Coast," *American Anthropologist* 25 (1923), pp. 1-20.

9 Ruth Benedict, *Patterns of Culture* (Mentor edition, copyright 1934), p. 174.

10 Goddard, *Indians of the Northwest Coast*, p. 13.

11 G. P. Murdock, *Our Primitive Contemporaries* (New York: Macmillan, 1934), p. 221

12 Ibid., p. 222.

13 Edward Sapir, "Central and North American Languages" (1929) in *Selected Writings* (Berkeley: University of California Press, 1939), p. 172.

14 Murdock, *Our Primitive Contemporaries*, p. 222.

15 Boas, "Tsimshian Mythology," pp. 393-477.

16 Murdock, *Our Primitive Contemporaries*, p. 227.

17 Ibid., pp. 227-29.

18 Ibid., p. 232.

19 Ibid., p. 233.

20 Ibid., p. 224.

21 Ibid., p. 223.

22 C. Darryl Forde, *Habitat, Economy and Society* (London: Methuen, 1934), p. 80.

23 Murdock, *Our Primitive Contemporaries*, p. 225.

24 Goddard, *Indians of the Northwest Coast*, p. 17.

25 Murdock, *Our Primitive Contemporaries*, pp. 235-36.

26 Ibid., pp. 235-36.

27 Ibid., p. 237.

28 Edward Sapir, "Social Organization of the West Coast Tribes," in *Selected Writings*, p. 472.

29 G. P. Murdock, "Rank and Potlatch Among the Haida," *Yale University Publications in Anthropology* 13 (1936).

30 Murdock, *Our Primitive Contemporaries*, p. 250.

31 Goddard, *Indians of the Northwest Coast*, p. 111.

32 Ibid.

33 Ibid., p. 112.

34 Murdock, *Our Primitive Contemporaries*, p. 236.

35 Boas, "Tsimshian Mythology," p. 512.

36 Murdock, *Our Primitive Contemporaries*, p. 248.

37 Ibid., p. 236.

38 Swanton, "Haida Texts and Myths," p. 286.

39 Ibid., p. 292.

40 Goddard, *Indians of the Northwest Coast,* p. 115.

41 Swanton, "Haida Texts and Myths," p. 190.

42 Ibid., p. 238.

43 Murdock, *Our Primitive Contemporaries,* p. 251.

CHAPTER III: VERSIONS OF THE MYTH

1   Stith Thompson, *The Folktale* (New York: Dryden, 1946), pp. 415-16.

2   Boas, "The Mythology and Folktales of the North American Indians," p. 457.

3   Ibid., pp. 458-59.

4   Stith Thompson, "Motif-Index of Folk Literature," *Indiana University Studies,* Vols. XIX-XXIII (Bloomington: 1936).

5   Antti Aarne, "The Types of the Folk-tale," Stith Thompson, trans. *FF Communications* No. 74 (Helsinki, 1928).

6   Boas, "Tsimshian Mythology," p. 949.

7   John Swanton, "Tlingit Myths and Texts," *Bureau of American Ethnology Bulletin* 39 (1909), pp. 55, 205.

8   Boas, "Tsimshian Mythology," p. 831.

9   Ibid., p. 607.

10 Ibid., p. 843.

11 Boas, "Dissemination of Tales Among the Natives of North America" (1891), in *Race, Language, and Culture,* p. 437.

12 Stith Thompson, *Tales of the North American Indians* (Cambridge: Harvard University Press, 1928), p. 356 n. 284.

13 Boas, "Dissemination of Tales Among the Natives of North America," pp. 441-42.

14 Thompson, *The Folktale,* p. 350. Also see *Tales of the North American Indians,* p. 135.

15 E. Sidney Hartland, *The Science of Fairy Tales* (New York: Scribners, 1891), p. 261.

16 Franz Boas, "Relationships Between Northwest America and Northeast Asia" (1933), *Race, Language, and Culture*, pp. 352-53.

17 *Asiatic Influences in American Folklore* (Kobenhavn, 1949), p. 95.

18 Waldemar Bogoros, "Tales of Yukaghir, Lamut, and Russianized Natives of Eastern Siberia," *Anthropological Papers of the American Museum of Natural History*, XX.1., p. 38.

19 Aarne, "The Types of the Folk-tale."

20 Thompson, "Motif Index of Folk Literature."

21 Thompson, *The Folktale*, pp. 423-25.

22 Mt=*Märchentype*, "type."

23 Goddard, *Indians of the Northwest Coast*, p. 111.

24 Thompson, *The Folktale*, p. 92.

25 Richard Burton (trans.), *The Arabian Nights* (Benares: The Kamashastra Society, 1885, 10 vols.), IV, p. 345.

26 J. A. MacCulloch, *Eddic Mythology* (Boston: Marshall Jones, 1930), p. 258.

27 L. Hibbard, *Medieval Romance in England* (New York: Oxford University Press, 1924), p. 240.

28 MacCulloch, *Eddic Mythology*, p. 262.

29 Masaharu Anesaki, *Japanese Mythology* (Boston: Marshall Jones, 1928), p. 258.

30 Herbert Giles, trans. (New York: Boni and Liveright, 1925), p. 364.

31 Hartland, *The Science of Fairy Tales*, p. 283.

32 Boas, "The Mythology and Folktales of the North American Indians," p. 490.

CHAPTER IV: SOURCES OF THE MYTH

1   Thompson, *The Folktale,* p. 93.

2   Ibid., p. 97.

3   This view of religion is propounded by Emile Durkheim in *Les Formes Elementaires de la Vie Religieuse* (Paris: 1912).

4   Sapir, *Selected Writings,* p. 351.

5   For a discussion of religion in terms of this dual-problem distinction, see Melville Herskovits, *Man and His Works* (New York: Knopf, 1947), pp. 347-78.

6   Sir James Frazer, *The Golden Bough.* One volume edition (New York: Macmillan, 1948, first edition 1890), p. 11.

7   Ibid., p. 12.

8   For discussions of Frazer's theory of magic, see Robert Lowie, *Primitive Religion* (New York: Boni & Liveright, 1924), pp. 136-50; and R. R. Marett, *Threshold of Religion* (London: Methuen, 1909). These books also criticize the "animism" theory propounded by Edward B. Tylor in *Primitive Culture* (London: 1871) and the "high god" theory of Andrew Lang's *Myth, Ritual, and Religion* (New York: Longmans Green, 1913, first published 1887, two vols.).

9   Franz Boas, "The Origin of Totemism" (1916), *Race, Language, and Culture,* p. 320.

10 Ibid., pp. 321-22.

11 Particularly *Ancient Society* (1877).

12 Friedrich Engels, *The Origin of the Family, Private Property and the State,* trans. by Ernest Untermann (Chicago: Charles H. Kerr Cooperative, 1902, first published in 1884), p. 68.

13 Heinrich Zimmer, *Myths and Symbols in Indian Art and Civilization* (New York: Pantheon, 1946), p. 96.

14 Ibid., p. 92.

15 Hartland, *The Science of Fairy Tales,* pp. 345-46.

16 MacCulloch, *Eddic Mythology,* pp. 258-59.

120

17 Thompson, *The Folktale*, p. 379.

18 Hibbard, *Medieval Romance in England*, p. 248.

19 Hartland, *The Science of Fairy Tales*, pp. 276-77.

20 It is necessary to mention Jessie Weston's *From Ritual to Romance* (New York: Peter Smith, 1941, first published 1920) as a work which preceded Loomis' study and pointed out these connections, but without his extensive documentation.

21 Roger S. Loomis, *Celtic Myth and Arthurian Romance* (New York: Columbia University Press, 1927), p. 290.

22 Ibid., p. 291.

23 Ibid., p. 301.

24 See Jane Ellen Harrison, *Prolegomena to the Study of Greek Religion* (Cambridge: Cambridge University Press, 1903) and *Themis* (Cambridge, 1912) for descriptions of ancient bird cults.

25 Robert Graves, *The White Goddess* (New York: Creative Age, 1948), p. 192. Emphasis mine. The Three Fates may in their turn be shown to be prototypes of the three witches in *Macbeth*. Whatever the faults of comparative study, it demonstrates the seldom realized complexity of the derivations and interrelationships of literary themes. Those who favor glorification of national literature might well profit by seeing the possible existence of historical relationship between elements of *Macbeth* and "He Who Hunted Birds in His Father's Village."

26 See Jane Ellen Harrison's *Ancient Art and Ritual* (New York: Holt, 1912) for a brief presentation of this view.

27 Boas, "The Mythology and Folktales of the North American Indians," p. 489.

28 Boas, "The Origin of Totemism," p. 317.

29 Ibid.

30 "The Explanatory Element in the Folk-Tales of the North American Indian," *Journal of American Folk Lore* XXVII (January-March, 1914), p. 24.

31 Thompson, *The Folktale*, p. 383.

32 Sapir, *Selected Writings,* p. 525.

33 Ibid., p. 527.

34 For a "pure" Freudian study, which has little relevance to the Swan-Maiden myth, see Otto Rank's *Myth of the Birth of the Hero* (New York: 1914).

35 Sapir, *Selected Writings,* p. 513.

36 C. G. Jung and C. Kerenyi, *Essays on a Science of Mythology* (New York: Pantheon, 1949), p. 100. For the standard statement of Jung's psychology see his *Psychology of the Unconscious* (New York: Moffat, Yard and Co., 1916).

37 Ibid., pp. 217-45.

38 See Jane Ellen Harrison's *Mythology* (Boston: Marshall Jones, 1924), pp. 59-128 for a description of this derivation.

39 Jung and Kerenyi, *Essays on a Science of Mythology,* p. 217.

40 Ibid., p. 220.

41 Ibid., p. 245.

42 Joseph Campbell, *The Hero with a Thousand Faces* (New York: Pantheon, 1948), p. 30. For a discussion of initiation rites, the standard work is Arnold Van Gennep's *Les Rites de Passage* (Paris, 1909).

43 This is possibly a misinterpretation of Zen satori. The prajna or sunyata schools of Mahayana may be closer to this type of enlightenment. (Added October 1957.)

44 Campbell, *The Hero with a Thousand Faces,* p. 29.

45 Ibid., pp. 120-21.

46 From John Swanton's article, "Some Practical Aspects of the Study of Myths," *Journal of American Folk Lore* XXIII (1910), p. 5.

47 Sapir, *Selected Wrtings,* p. 527.

CHAPTER V: THE MYTH AS LITERATURE

1 For example, the fact of matrilineal descent in ancient Crete

and contemporary Haida culture, although suggesting similarity at first blush, has virtually no significance, as the institution plays different roles in the two cultures.

2   Jung and Kerenyi, *Essays on a Science of Mythology,* p. 219n.

3   Graves, *The White Goddess,* p. x.

4   Ibid., p. 10.

5   Campbell, *The Hero with a Thousand Faces,* p. 3.

6   Franz Boas, "The Folklore of the Eskimo" (1904), in *Race, Language, and Culture,* p. 511.

7   W. R. Bascom, "Western Africa and the Complexity of Primitive Cultures," *American Anthropologist,* 50 (1948).

8   Paul Radin, *Literary Aspects of North American Mythology* (Ottowa: Government Printing Bureau, 1915), pp. 1-2.

9   Ibid., p. 7.

10   Ibid., p. 26.

11   Ibid., p. 9.

12   Waterman, "The Explanatory Element in the Folktales of the North American Indians," p. 41.

13   For a discussion of North American Indian poetry, see A. Grove Day's *The Sky Clears* (New York: Macmillan, 1951), pp. 1-34.

14   Franz Boas, "Stylistic Aspects of Primitive Literature" (1925), in *Race, Language, and Culture,* p. 491.

15   Edward Sapir, "Song Recitative in Paiute Mythology" (1925), *Selected Writings,* p. 463.

16   Ibid., p. 464.

17   Ibid., p. 466.

18   Franz Boas, "Literature, Music, and Dance" in (Boas, ed.) *General Anthropology* (New York: D. C. Heath, 1938. War Department Edition), p. 591.

19   Boas, "Stylistic Aspects," p. 491.

20 Melville Jacobs and Bernhard Stern, *Outline of Anthropology* (New York: Barnes and Noble, n.d.), p. 224.

21 Ibid., p. 225.

22 Ibid., p. 226.

23 Paul Radin, *Literary Elements in North American Mythology*, pp. 42-43.

24 Paul Radin, *Primitive Man as Philosopher* (New York: Appleton, 1927), p. 5.

25 Paul Radin, *Primitive Religion* (New York: Viking, 1937). p. 21.

26 Boas, "Mythology and Folktales of the North American Indians," p. 482.

27 This myth actually is lost forever to any literary comprehension. The Haida at present have virtually no oral tradition left. Even when Swanton collected this myth in 1904, only a few aged informants were available. My point is merely the theoretical possibility of a Westerner's understanding it.

28 Bernard Bosanquet, "The Esthetic Attitude and Its Embodiments," in (Melvin Rader, ed.) *A Modern Book of Aesthetics* (New York: Holt, 1935), p. 5.

29 Sapir, "Central and North American Languages," pp. 174-75.

30 From the Phonetic Key in Swanton's "Tlingit Myths and Texts," p. viii.

31 Swanton, "Haida Texts and Myths," p. 7.

32 Franz Boas, "Metaphorical Expression in the Language of the Kwakiutl Indians" (1920), in *Race, Language, and Culture,* p. 239.

33 I. A. Richards, *Mencius on the Mind* (New York: Harcourt and Brace, 1932), p. 87.

34 Ibid., p. 93.

35 Ibid., p. 98.

36 Bronislaw Malinowski, "The Problem of Meaning in Primitive Languages" (1923), in *Magic, Science, and Religion* (Glencoe:

The Free Press, 1948), p. 238.

37 I. A. Richards, *Principles of Literary Criticism* (New York: Harcourt and Brace, 1949, first published 1923), p. 267.

38 Radin, *Primitive Religion*, p. 102.

39 Campbell, *The Hero with a Thousand Faces*, p. 100.

40 Ibid., p. 101.

41 Richards, *Principles of Literary Criticism*, p. 181.

42 Maud Bodkin's *Archetypal Patterns in Poetry* (London: Oxford, 1934) discusses the persistence of mythic imagery in conscious written poetry, and the relation of the poet to his archetypal material.

43 "The Style of the Mythical Age," introduction to Rachel Bespaloff's *On the Iliad* (New York: Pantheon, 1947), p. 10.

44 Ibid., p. 11.

45 Ibid., p. 13.

46 Northrop Frye, "The Archetypes of Literature," in *Kenyon Review*, Winter, 1951, p. 101.

47 Henry James, *The Figure in the Carpet* (1896).

CHAPTER VI: FUNCTION OF THE MYTH

1 Reprinted in *Magic, Science, and Religion*, pp. 72-124.

2 Ibid., p. 78.

3 Ibid., p. 79.

4 Mark Schorer, *William Blake* (New York: Holt, 1949), p. 27.

5 Ibid., p. 29. Perhaps Schorer's "indispensable ingredient of all culture" is a misquoting of Malinowski's "vital ingredient of all human civilization."

6 Robert Lowie, *History of Ethnological Theory* (New York: Rinehart, 1937), p. 238.

7 Jung and Kerenyi, *Essays on a Science of Mythology*, p. 7.

8   Ibid., p. 9. Greek letters in the text.

9   Ibid., p. 11.

10 I. A. Richards, *Coleridge on the Imagination* (London: Kegan Paul, 1934), pp. 171-72.

11 *The Individual and His Society* (New York: Columbia University Press, 1939).

12 *The Psychological Frontiers of Society* (New York: Columbia University Press, 1945).

13 Ibid., p. 29.

14 Ibid., p. 34.

15 Ibid., p. 40.

16 Ibid., p. 96. Thus one might see the Haida Swan-Maiden myth as a projection of a male sense of inferiority to women, coupled with a distrust of the mother. Woman is portrayed as having supernatural attributes and the power to go and come at will. The hero's loss of the maiden is a projection of the childhood loss of mother; the reunion in the sky is a wish-fulfillment projection which proves unsatisfactory—leaving the hero no recourse but to become a seagull (infantile regression). Since there is no way of checking this against Haida child training, such interpretation is idle.

17 Ibid., p. 39.

18 Ibid., p. 45.

19 Ibid., p. 39n.

20 The identity of the human community and the universe in ancient Near East mythology has been studied by H. Frankfort, H. A. Frankfort, Wilson, and Jacobsen in *Before Philosophy* (Penguin Edition, 1949. First published as *The Intellectual Adventure of Ancient Man* [Chicago: University of Chicago Press, 1946]).

21 Campbell, *The Hero with a Thousand Faces,* p. 364.

22 Frazer, *The Golden Bough,* p. 244. Frazer's patronizing attitude toward preliterate peoples, which has annoyed many anthropologists, may be seen here.

23 Malinowski, "Meaning in Primitive Languages," pp. 258-59.

24 Ernst Cassirer, *Language and Myth* (New York: Harpers, 1946), p. 84.

25 A. L. Kroeber, *Anthropology* (New York: Harcourt and Brace, 1923, revised edition 1949), p. 225.

26 George Santayana, *The Sense of Beauty* (New York: Scribners, 1896, reprinted 1936), p. 107.

27 *Philosophy in a New Key* (New York: Mentor edition, copyright 1942).

28 Ibid., p. 16.

29 Sapir, *Selected Writings*, p. 568.

30 Rene Wellek and Austen Warren, *Theory of Literature* (Harcourt and Brace, 1942), p. 198.

31 T. S. Eliot, " 'Ulysses,' Order and Myth" (1923), reprinted in Schorer, Miles, and McKenzie (editors), *Criticism* (New York: Harcourt and Brace, 1948), p. 270.

32 Philip Wheelwright, "Poetry, Myth, and Reality," in (Allen Tate, ed.) *The Language of Poetry* (Princeton University Press, 1942), p. 33.

33 John Ciardi (ed.), *Mid-Century American Poets* (New York: Twayne, 1950), p. 27.

34 Graves, *The White Goddess*, p. 373.

35 Campbell, *The Hero with a Thousand Faces*, p. 391.

BIBLIOGRAPHY

Aarne, Antti. "The Types of the Folk-tale." Translated by Stith Thompson. *FF Communications No. 74.* Helsinki: 1928.

Anesaki, Masaharu. *Japanese Mythology.* Mythology of All Races, vol. VIII. Boston: Marshall Jones, 1928.

Bascom, William. "Western Africa and the Complexity of Primitive Cultures," *American Anthropologist* 50 (1948).

Benedict, Ruth. *Patterns of Culture.* Mentor edition, 1934.

Bespaloff, Rachel. *On the Iliad.* With an Introduction by Hermann Broch. New York: Pantheon, 1947.

Boas, Franz. "Tsimshian Mythology." In *Thirty-first Report of the Bureau of American Ethnology* (1909-1910).

_____ . *Race, Language, and Culture.* New York: Macmillan, 1949. Copyright 1940.

_____ . Editor. *General Anthropology.* New York: Heath, 1938

Bodkin, Maud. *Archetypal Patterns in Poetry.* London: Oxford, 1934.

Bogoras, Waldemar. "Tales of Yukaghir, Lamut, and Russianized Natives of Eastern Siberia." *Anthropological Papers of the American Museum of Natural History,* XX.1 (1918).

Burton, Richard. Translator. *The Arabian Nights.* Benares: The Kamashastra Society, 1885. 10 vols.

Campbell, Joseph. *The Hero with a Thousand Faces.* New York: Pantheon, 1949.

Ciardi, John. Editor. *Mid-Century American Poets.* New York: Twayne, 1950.

Durkheim, Emile. *Les Formes Elementaires de la Vie Religieuse.* Paris: 1912.

Eliot, T. S. "Ulysses, Order and Myth." In *Criticism,* edited by Mark Schorer, Josephine Miles, and Gordon MacKenzie. New York: Harcourt and Brace, 1948.

Engels, Friedrich. *The Origin of the Family, Private Property, and the State.* Chicago: Charles H. Kerr Co. Cooperative, 1902. (First published 1884.)

Forde, C. Darryl. *Habitat, Economy, and Society.* London: Methuen, 1934.

Frankfort, Henri et al. *Before Philosophy.* Penguin edition, 1949. (Originally published as *The Intellectual Adventure of Ancient Man.* Chicago: University of Chicago Press, 1946.)

Frazer, Sir James G. *The Golden Bough.* One volume edition. New York: Macmillan, 1948. (First edition, 1890; third edition in 12 volumes, London: 1911-1915.)

Frye, Northrop. "The Archetypes of Literature." *Kenyon Review,* vol. XIII (Winter, 1951), pp. 92-109.

Goddard, Pliny Earl. *Indians of the Northwest Coast.* American Museum of Natural History Handbook, 1924.

Graves, Robert. *The White Goddess.* New York: Creative Age, 1948.

Harrison, Jane Ellen. *Prolegomena to the Study of Greek Religion.* Cambridge: Cambridge University Press, 1903.

_____ . *Themis.* Cambridge, 1912.

_____ . *Ancient Art and Ritual.* New York: Holt, 1913.

_____ . *Mythology.* Boston: Marshall Jones, 1924.

Hartland, E. Sidney. *The Science of Fairy-tales.* New York: Scribners, 1891.

Hatt, Gudmund. *Asiatic Influences in American Folklore.* Kobenhavn, 1949.

Herskovits, Melville. *Man and His Works.* New York: Knopf, 1949.

Hibbard, L. *Mediaeval Romance in England.* New York: Oxford University Press, 1924.

Jacobs, Melville, and Stern, Bernhard. *Outline of Anthropology.* New York: Barnes and Noble, 1947.

Jung, C. G. *Psychology of the Unconscious.* New York: Moffat and Yard, 1916.

_____ . and Kerenyi, C. *Essays in a Science of Mythology.* New York: Pantheon, 1949.

Kardiner, Abram. *The Individual and His Society.* New York: Columbia University Press, 1939.

_____ . *The Psychological Frontiers of Society.* New York: Columbia University Press, 1945.

Kroeber, A. L. *Anthropology.* New York: Harcourt and Brace, revised edition, 1949. (Copyright 1923.)

_____ . "American Culture and the Northwest Coast." *American Anthropologist,* 25 (1923), pp. 1-20.

Lang, Andrew. *Myth, Ritual, and Religion.* London: Longmans and Green, 1913, Two volumes. (First published in 1887.)

Langer, Susanne K. *Philosophy in a New Key.* Penguin edition, copyright 1942.

Loomis, Roger S. *Celtic Myth and Arthurian Romance.* New York: Columbia University Press, 1926.

Lowie, Robert. *Primitive Religion.* New York: Boni and Liveright, 1924.

_____ . *The History of Ethnological Theory.* New York: Rinehart, 1937.

MacCulloch, John Arnott. *Eddic Mythology.* Mythology of All Races, vol. 2. Boston: Marshall Jones, 1930.

Malinowski, Bronislaw. *Magic, Science, and Religion.* Glencoe: The Free Press, 1948.

Marett, R. R. *Threshold of Religion.* London: Methuen, 1909.

Morgan, Lewis Henry, *Ancient Society.* 1877.

Murdock, George Peter. *Our Primitive Contemporaries.* New York: Macmillan, 1934.

_____ . "Rank and Potlatch Among the Haida." Yale University Publications in Anthropology 13 (1936).

Rader, Melvin. Editor. *A Modern Book of Esthetics.* New York: Holt, 1935.

Radin, Paul. *Literary Aspects of North American Mythology.* Ottawa: Government Printing Bureau, 1915.

_____ . *Primitive Man as Philosopher.* New York: Appleton, 1927.

_____ . *Primitive Religion.* New York: Viking, 1937.

Rank, Otto. *The Myth of the Birth of the Hero.* New York: 1914.

Richards, I. A. *Principles of Literary Criticism.* New York: Harcourt and Brace, 1949. (First published 1923.)

_____ . *Mencius on the Mind.* New York: Harcourt and Brace, 1932.

_____ . *Coleridge on the Imagination.* London: Kegan Paul, 1934.

Santayana, George. *The Sense of Beauty.* New York: Scribners, 1896.

Schorer, Mark. *William Blake.* New York: Holt, 1946.

Swanton, John. "Haida Texts and Myths." *Bureau of American Ethnology Bulletin* 29 (1905).

_____ . "Tlingit Myths and Texts." *Bureau of American Ethnology Bulletin* 39 (1909).

_____ . "Some Practical Aspects of the Study of Myths." *Journal of American Folklore* XXIII.5 (1910).

Thompson, Stith. *The Folktale.* New York: Dryden Press, 1946.

_____ . "Motif Index of Folk Literature." Indiana University Studies, vols. XIX-XXIII. Bloomington, 1936.

_____ . *Tales of the North American Indians.* Cambridge: Harvard University Press, 1928.

Thomson, George. *Marxism and Poetry.* New York: International, 1946.

Tylor, E. B. *Primitive Culture.* London: 1871.

Van Gennep, Arnold. *Les Rites de Passage.* Paris: 1909.

_____ . *La Formation des Legendes.* Paris: 1910.

Waterman, T. T. "The Explanatory Element in the Folktales of the North American Indians." *Journal of American Folklore* 27 (1914).

Wellek, Rene, and Warren, Austin. *Theory of Literature.* New York: Harcourt and Brace, 1942.

Weston, Jessie. *From Ritual to Romance.* New York: Peter Smith, 1941. (First published 1920.)

Wheelwright, Philip. "Poetry, Myth, and Reality." In *The Language of Poetry.* Edited by Allen Tate. Princeton: Princeton University Press, 1942.

Wissler, Clark. *The American Indian.* New York: Oxford University Press, 1938.

Zimmer, Heinrich. *Myths and Symbols in Indian Art and Civilization.* New York: Pantheon, 1946.

GREY FOX BOOKS